Help Desk Management
How to run a computer user support Service Desk effectively

By Wayne Schlicht

Introduction

Customers deserve a world-class Help Desk

It is time to build a successful Help Desk team. Successful Help Desk teams have similar attributes in common. The management, people, and process structure set successful teams apart from teams with performance issues. If your team needs some improvement, this book can immediately help. I wrote this book for new and experienced managers trying to build award-winning customer-focused teams. This book is not based on abstract theories. The recommendations I share with you are based on real-life experiences building successful customer-focused teams. Through trial and error, I am sharing what worked for my team and what can work for your team. I am confident you will find this information helpful for you to improve your management skills and your team's engagement. Let's set you on a successful path to building a truly great team.

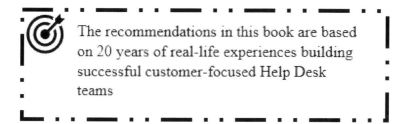

The recommendations in this book are based on 20 years of real-life experiences building successful customer-focused Help Desk teams

Solid management practices based on industry-standard processes are critical for an efficient, well-performing, and customer-focused Help Desk. The challenge for a manager is to know what those industry standards are and how to introduce them to your team. I have assembled specific topics based on the essential industry best practices. I teach each subject and explain what they are and how they will benefit your team.

Easy step by step approach

Many of the topics introduced in this book will include straight forward, step-by-step approach for you to implement and mature your IT and Help Desk services. Most of the principles in this book not only apply to Help Desk, call center, and information technology teams but also fit well with management principles in any type of team or organization. In this book, my goal is to empower you to build the right staff following industry-standard processes leveraging the right technology to deliver award-winning services.

Quick start implementation worksheets

Once you completely understand the process, chapters are concluded with a quick start implementation worksheet to put your new process into action. These quick-start implementation worksheets are in Word and follow a step-by-step sequencing. All quick start implement worksheets can also be downloaded from the companion resource website BuildaHelpDesk.com in PDF form!

Companion Resource Website BuildaHelpDesk.com

In this book, I refer to many resources such as a Help Desk maturity assessment and quick-start implementation worksheets. I have made available downloadable content and resources at the book's companion resource website, BuildaHelpDesk.com, in the Help Desk Management book section.

Something for every experience level

If you are a new Help Desk Manager, you will appreciate the beginner to an intermediate level foundational overview of each topic. This foundational overview will provide you with baseline information, which you can use to compare your team's policies, procedures, and work practices. Once you identify your gaps, we offer improvement suggestions and identify key steps to implement them. To simplify the process, we provide design worksheets for most topics to use as a guide. If you have experience as a manager and are looking to mature your team's services, you will also find more advanced information throughout the book.

The book at a glance

Help Desk Foundation Section

Chapter 1: Help Desk Management – If you like technology and helping people, find out why Help Desk management can be a fun and rewarding career. Help desk management is all about customer service. It's about working with people, helping them solve their problems, and getting them back up and running again. In this chapter, we will discuss the details of Help Desk management.

Chapter 2: Perform a Help Desk maturity assessment - A maturity assessment is a tool used by companies to determine their maturity compared to industry standards. Learn how to set up a Help Desk maturity assessment to understand how they are doing and what needs attention for improvement.

Chapter 3: Implementing Help Desk Improvement Projects – A well-funded Help Desk is a crucial factor in being responsive to the company user's technology needs. However, resources are not unlimited. Find out how to target resources for improvements where they will make the most significant impact on the people, process, and technology areas.

Chapter 4: Create a Mission Statement - A mission statement is the cornerstone of your company by communicating its purpose. It defines the reason your company exists, what it does, and how it does it. We help you create a department mission statement that incorporates your company's goals, objectives, and values.

Chapter 5: Employee and Customer Support Structure - We will review the factors, rules, and policies to consider when you design your Help Desk employee support structure. We will also review the Help Desk customer support structure, which determines how customers are handled and how information flows within the Help

Desk department. These decisions include defining contact channels used, hours of operation, the language supported, customer base location, security practices, and many other items.

Help Desk People Section

Chapter 6: Understand your team - One of the biggest challenges for a new manager is understanding their team. Every company has unique organizational structures, job descriptions, use of specialists, and staff to management ratios. If you recognize and study the efficiencies of these structures and processes, you can make informed decisions for improvements. We help you make positive improvements to increase productivity, reduce costs, and improve the overall work-life balance.

Chapter 7: Job Descriptions - One of the best ways to understand the current expectations of your staff is to review their role's job description. We discuss what a well-defined job description should include and why it is critical to define the primary functions and duties of the position.

Chapter 8: Meet with your staff - It is essential to build a productive relationship with your team and set expectations early. This chapter covers topics such as the initial meeting, daily stand-up meetings, setting up weekly meetings, one on one sessions, skip-level meetings, career path discussions, and employee recognition.

Chapter 9: Helpful Certifications for a Help Desk Agent - Many technology application and service companies offer certifications for their systems and applications. Employee certifications recognize an employee's accumulated training and experience in a subject area. This chapter covers some of the most important certifications for Help Desk personnel.

Chapter 10: Implementing an Employee Training and Development Program - Good employee training and development programs don't just happen. Learn the core components of what makes up a highly effective employee training and development program. This chapter includes a discussion about trainers, curriculum, onboarding, just-in-time, and ongoing training.

Help Desk Process Section

Chapter 11: Identity and Access Management - Identity and access management ensures the right people have the appropriate access to systems and applications to perform their work when they require it. A Help Desk plays a significant role in the identity and access management process. We will discuss the Help Desk agent's job duties and essential identity and access management projects to implement.

Chapter 12: Help Desk Phone System - A phone system is the mainstay of all support channels, and it is critical you have a foundational knowledge of how your system is set up and what options are enabled.

Chapter 13: Implementing a quality assurance audit program - Ensure Help Desk agents are providing high-quality customer service. We will discuss how to implement and run a quality assurance audit program by reviewing calls and tickets on a regular schedule using a standard methodology.

Chapter 14: Improve First Contact Resolution (FCR) - First contact resolution (FCR) is the percentage of customer contacts (incidents) that are solved by the Help Desk in the initial customer interaction without interruption. FCR is one of the essential Help Desk measurements and directly ties into staffing, cost, and customer satisfaction. Learn how to measure, control, and improve your team's FCR rate.

Chapter 15: Implement Performance Reporting - Learn what the vital Help Desk key performance indicators (KPI) are and how they are used by management to understand how the team is performing. We cover essential steps to ensure you are capturing accurate data to measure, manage, and implement continuous improvement efforts.

Chapter 16: Social Media Strategies - Customers are using social media to ask technical questions, complain about products or services, and report outages or service interruptions. Understand how Help Desk social media strategies can be used to monitor and respond more effectively to your customers actively.

Chapter 17: Help Desk Ticket Classification - Every Help Desk needs a ticket classification scheme to properly handle the customer's issues when they contact the Help Desk for support. Applying proper ticket classification immediately when a Help Desk ticket is created enables the Help Desk Agent to leverage more advanced resolution allowing tools.

Chapter 18: Design a Call Volume Management Strategy - In this chapter, we will be discussing how to reduce or modify inbound call volume. Help Desk Managers will employ strategies to reduce or alter inbound call volumes to solve specific issues. We will discuss those issues and solutions you can use.

Chapter 19: Implement a Shift-Left Support Strategy – Understand how a shift-left customer support strategy can reduce costs, improve resolution times, and empower your customers. Shift-left is based on the customer on the far left and SME engineers on the far right. I will guide you in the process of shifting customer support closer to the customer.

Help Desk Customer Section

Chapter 20: Learn the Business - To be effect supporting a business, you must understand the business. By knowing your company's business, products, and applications, you can begin to prioritize incidents, manage changes, and better support your customer's needs. Successful managers know it is essential to quickly build relationships and seek input from key stakeholder groups to be successful. Careers are built on a foundation of communications and strong relationships. Learn how to quickly build relationships and collaborate with key stakeholders of your support department to be successful.

Chapter 21: Marketing the Help Desk - The services offered by your Help Desk have value only if they are being consumed. The customers of your Help Desk need to know what services are available and how to request them. Learn how to get started marketing the Help Desk.

Chapter 22: Typical Customer Issues - Customers are the lifeblood of the company. Understanding why your customers call the Help Desk and what are the most frequently occurring questions and issues will help you improve the customer experience. We identify the top 10 customer support issues and recommendations on how to handle them.

Chapter 23: Customer Service Complaints - We identify the most common Help Desk customer service issues and recommendations on how to handle them.

Chapter 24: Total Contact Ownership - The principle of Total Contact Ownership is whoever takes the first customer issue will own the incident until it has been resolved. This chapter covers the benefits of Total Contact Ownership to ensure customer issues are addressed and resolved in a timely satisfying manner.

Help Desk and IT Service Management Section

Chapter 25: Incident Management Best Practices - An incident is an event not part of the standard operation of the service, causing an interruption to the quality of the service. The goal of Incident Management is to return the service to standard functionality quickly while minimizing the impact on the business. This chapter discusses the components of an incident management program and best practices to implement a program that works for your team and company.

Chapter 26: Major Incident Management Best Practices - Designing a major incident management process is critical to protecting a company from significant financial loss, tarnishing its reputation, and impacting its customers. In this chapter, we will discuss what a major incident is, discuss the phases of the lifecycle, and review the best practices you need to know to succeed.

Chapter 27: Service Requests – Service request fulfillment is the process of provisioning IT Services to the customer. A service request can be customers requesting system access, information, or a standard low-risk change to be fulfilled. We discuss the process and best practices for service request fulfillment.

Chapter 28: Event Management - Event management is the process of monitoring IT services to ensure they are performing well. Event management can help you respond to incidents faster. By implementing an effective event management program, your IT systems will be more available.

Chapter 29: Problem Management - Problem management is the life cycle process of identifying, investigating, documenting, and permanently resolving incidents causing problems in the production environment. Problem management is focused on identifying the incident's root cause and preventing the recurrence of service-impacting incidents.

Chapter 30: Change management - Change management is about managing the IT system change lifecycle with standardized processes and proper oversight. Properly implemented, a mature IT change control process will minimize the negative impact on customers, IT services, and operations.

Chapter 31: Give your Knowledgebase some Wisdom - A robust and mature Knowledge Management System enables the Help Desk to deliver greater business value with more efficiency. This chapter outlines the process of starting or maturing a knowledge management system.

Help Desk Resources and Important Links – We assembled a list of essential resources and links for your benefit.

Help Desk Foundation Section

In the Help Desk Foundation section, we will discuss some of the basic properties of the Help Desk. First, we will discuss Help Desk management. We will discuss what it is and the benefits. Next, we will discuss why it is crucial not only to have a Help Desk but to fund it adequately. Then we will move on to discuss the mission statement, its importance, and the benefits. Finally, we will cover the organizational and support structure of a world-class Help Desk. This foundational knowledge of the Help Desk is essential and will be followed up by specific areas of expertise related to the Help Desk.

Chapter 1

Help Desk Management Best Practices

Help Desk management is a fun and rewarding career if you like technology and helping people. Help desk management is all about customer service. It's about working with people, helping them solve their problems, and getting them back up and running again. In addition to the Help Desk Manager role, there are many positions that are associated with Help Desk Management. These positions include the overall IT Director, Help Desk Supervisors, and team leads. The Help Desk management team is also surrounded by agents that feel the same way. The Help Desk staff loves to help people with their technology-related issues. To be a successful Help Desk Manager, you must manage the people, the process, and technology.

 One of the essential ingredients of an effective Help Desk is the people. Finding the right people for the Help Desk does not just happen. It starts by creating a Help Desk job description that accurately reflects the position requirements and your expectations. We will cover how to create an effective Help Desk job description. Once you hire the right people, you must train them properly. Employee training starts with an excellent new employee onboarding process. One of the more effective Help Desk I helped create was a 6-week new employee onboarding process. By the end of the six weeks of training, the Help Desk agent was ready to take live calls and performed very well. While new employee onboarding training is essential, it's only the beginning of training. We will cover how to create an ongoing effective training and development program for your staff.

To create an outstanding help desk, you need a mature performance management program. One of the components of a performance management program is a quality assurance audit program for calls and tickets. We will show you how to build an agent scorecard to provide a comprehensive review of the agent's performance. Only by listening to the agent's interaction with the customer and reviewing the support ticket documentation can you understand how well your staff is performing. As a result of the program, you'll see increased positive behavior and a reduction in inappropriate behavior. Finally, you will have a meaningful annual review process.

In addition to managing your staff, you must manage the customers. To manage customers properly, you must learn the business that you're supporting. It's essential to build relationships as a Help Desk manager. You must identify who the key stakeholders are. You also must understand what's important to the stakeholders. With customers, there are always complaints. So, managing complaints and dealing with customers requires a calm and logical approach. All these subjects we will cover in-depth.

As a Help Desk manager, you do have to put great processes in place to manage the people effectively. These processes and controls also ensure that the customer's satisfaction stays high and the expectations are met. These processes include how to increase first contact resolution, how to perform a maturity assessment on the help desk, and how to report metrics effectively. We will also discuss ITIL processes and how the Help Desk plays a major role in ensuring they are effective.

So, with that said, what are some of the major Help Desk Management best practices we will be covering in this book? We will focus on Help

Desk Management best practices core areas based on industry standards and universally accepted practices. Each one of these best practices categories includes people, process, technology, and IT service management principles.

Top 10 Help Desk Management Best Practices

1. Assess your maturity against industry standards.
2. Understand the business and the customer's expectations.
3. Implement fair and consistent policies.
4. Implement repeatable support procedures.
5. Use effective and accurate job descriptions.
6. Invest in employee training, development, and certifications.
7. Understand your budget and reduce costs.
8. Implement performance management practices to improve quality.
9. Create a support structure that empowers customers' effectiveness and efficiency.
10. Ensure the Help Desk is an effective partner in your company's overall IT Service Management plan.

Is your top 10 list different? I would like to hear from you. Visit the Help Desk Management resource website at https://buildahelpdesk.com/ to provide your feedback.

Let's get started building a world-class Help Desk!

Chapter 2

Help Desk Maturity Assessment

> **Chapter Objectives**
> - Benefits of a Help Desk maturity assessment.
> - Learn the core focus areas of a maturity assessment.
> - Understand how a maturity assessment grades the maturity of your Help Desk.
> - Complete a maturity assessment.

For an organization initially setting up its Help Desk, there is a lot of industry-standard process information available to build a strong foundation. If you have an established Help Desk, you can have your current processes and practices assessed against these industry standards. This will assist the Help Desk manager to understand how they are doing and what needs attention for improvement. In the IT Service Management community, we start by using something called a maturity assessment. A maturity assessment is a tool used by companies to determine their maturity compared to industry standards. Sometimes a maturity assessment is referred to as a gap assessment. It is important to note that the value realized from performing an assessment is directly related to the thoroughness of the assessment data gathered, which includes staff interviews. There are many benefits to completing a maturity assessment

In addition to the information provided in this book, there is a lot of the information supplied on the book's resource website. Included with the Help Desk information is an IT Help Desk maturity assessment. To try the maturity assessment, click the following link.

Important Link: Build a Help Desk's maturity assessment. Visit and take your IT Help Desk Maturity Assessment today!
https://buildahelpdesk.com/help-desk-maturity-assessment-guide/

Help Desk maturity assessment benefits

Funding justification – Assessment results are frequently used to justify funding of improvement initiatives and projects. An analysis and recommendation from an independent group usually carry a lot of influence.

Cost reduction – By implementing process improvement recommendations from an assessment, teams can become more efficient. Efficiency gains can lead to consuming fewer resources and an overall cost reduction.

Customer service experience improvements - Customer service experience improvements are frequently realized when the Help Desk implements more mature processes. A mature process is a process that is repeatable and has an outcome that will be positive a high percentage of the time.

Productivity Gains – Ad hoc processes tend to consume a lot of time and resources. When Help Desk agents have efficient and well-thought-out processes, the team will experience increased resource productivity.

Future Growth – When processes are defined, managed, and optimized, it leads to departments being able to increase their scale. Scalable support processes will support future business growth.

Compliance – Chaotic and reactive support processes can be difficult to audit and lead to more frequent compliance violations. Mature processes have a firm adherence to governance and compliance regulations.

Maturity Assessment Core Focus Areas

A maturity assessment for the Help Desk will focus on critical areas to gather information. The core focus areas of a maturity and gap assessment can vary between assessment vendors, but they all have similar focus areas. Below are examples of focus areas that will be assessed.

Leadership & Management Leadership and management play a significant role in the assessed maturity level. Employees thrive when leadership and management are supportive of them and give them the tools so they can do their job. Assessment will look at controls and governance.

Organizational Structure - The organization or structure of a company is also fundamental. A maturity assessment will look at how decisions are made. A project management maturity assessment will analyze how projects are created, controlled, and implemented. A maturity assessment will review how the department is structured, how teams are managed, and how performance is maintained.

Employee Engagement Nothing can hurt a company's performance like employees are disengaged. Employee engagement is a critical factor in the success of a company. Measuring how engaged employees are is a vital part of a maturity assessment.

Customer Experience As with any other department, the help desk is measured by how well the customer is treated. Customer satisfaction is lucky Focus on a maturity assessment for the help desk. It will look at the processes in place in the flow of the customer and their experience with the help desk.

Policies & Procedures – These are formal documents providing the high-level operational framework within which the Help Desk functions. A policy is expressed in broad terms and governs what, why, how, when, and to who the Help Desk services are provided. Procedures are the detailed instructions to carry it out. Policies and procedures will be compared against industry standards and assessed for their maturity level.

Technology The technology used at the help desk is also critical. You don't need the most expensive equipment, but you need adequate equipment. Does the help desk have the proper technology in place to meet the challenges that they face? An assessment will review the technology being used and provide a good recommendation.

Metrics and Reporting – Not only are metrics and reporting critical to measure the performance level of the Help Desk, but it's also essential to support the business decisions. A review of the metrics and reporting are part of the assessment. Recommendations will include how to improve this going forward.

Security Maturity Assessment – Security compliance with industry standards is always a major focus during an assessment. One area an assessment will focus on is password management procedures. Does the Help Desk validate the requestor's identity using security challenge questions or other means? Are changes or resets to enterprise application accounts passwords tracked and audited? Is there a self-service password management method available to users? These are just some of the security maturity assessment areas focused on when determining the maturity level.

Maturity Assessment Scale

A maturity assessment has defined categories and standards. These categories and standards will help the assessor compare the Help Desk's core areas of people, process, technology, governance, and controls against industry standards. All assessments will use a maturity assessment scale to rank each of these core areas. Numbers from the scale are used to assign a maturity level of the Help Desk operations. Some assessments use a scale of four levels, five levels, or even up to eight levels. The most accepted assessment scale level of maturity in the industry is five levels.

Maturity Level 1 – A maturity level of 1 is your basic level. It means you're just starting or at a foundational level. This level indicates there are no fundamental processes in place. There is little or no documentation on support processes in place. No automation is being used. Activities are not repeatable and can be described as ad hoc. The work environment of the team is chaotic, and the customers are not getting what they're expecting. No reporting exists, or it is very minimal.

Maturity Level 2 – A maturity level of 2 means that there are some processes that are starting to be put in place, but they're not very mature. Most of the support activities are documented but have not been improved regularly. There may be some automation used, but it is siloed. Many activities are repeatable to a point, but some level of still ad hoc still exists. At this level, the employees will feel like their processes are reactive. They are firefighting issues, and whatever occurs, they are trying to figure it out as they go. Reporting exists, and a few reports are used to assist with decisions.

Maturity Level 3 – At a maturity level of 3, the help desk is becoming more proactive. Their processes are documented and are reviewed occasionally for improvements. Automated systems are in use and centrally managed. The employees feel more empowered to make suggestions for improvement. The recommendations for improvement are implemented. Customers feel like they are starting to get things that they expect. Reporting at this level is functional and is used to make decisions.

Maturity Level 4 - At a maturity level of 4, decisions are being made by metrics and reports. Centrally managed automation is feeding output data to refine the process further. Processes are being optimized, customers are feeling important, and continuous Improvement is very effective.

Maturity Level 5 – a maturity level of five signifies that everything is exceptional. There's real value to the business. All processes are continuously improved, expectations are being met, everything is optimizing, and there's a real value for the company. Automation is using AI to learn, improve, and accelerate more refined processes. Self-service services are widely used. Knowledge is shared and used throughout the company.

Help Desk Maturity Assessment Worksheet

A maturity assessment is a tool used by companies to determine their maturity compared to industry standards. Below we recommend the following steps to determine your Help Desk's maturity level.

Step 1 – Take the Help Desk Maturity Assessment

Visit the Help Desk Management book's companion resource website and complete the Help Desk maturity assessment. To try the IT Help Desk Maturity Assessment, click the following link.

https://buildahelpdesk.com/help-desk-maturity-assessment-guide/

Alternatively, you can go to BuildaHelpDesk.com a search for the keywords "Maturity Assessment."

Step 2 – Review the assessment results

Once you have completed the Help Desk maturity assessment, the results will be emailed to you. The results will give you your overall maturity level from a one to a five, with five being the most mature. You will also receive specific maturity levels for each of the ten core areas of your Help Desk's operations.

Step 3 – Create an improvement plan for low assessment maturity results.

The IT Help Desk Maturity Assessment results will list ten core areas with a maturity level for each. The maturity level will be in the range of 1 (basic) to 5 (very mature). Review the assessment results for any category with a maturity level of 1 or 2. Categories with low maturity levels offer the best opportunities for improvement. Using the information from this book and the resource website, create an improvement plan for all categories with a maturity level of 1 or 2.

Chapter 3

Implementing Help Desk Improvement Projects

Having an internal and well-funded Help Desk is an essential factor in building an Information Technology (IT) department that is responsive to the company user's technology needs. Having an internal Help Desk gives IT management the most control of the customer experience. Unlike an outsourced Help Desk, an internal Help Desk has a better understanding of the unique IT environment of a company. Since an internal Help Desk is made up of employees, they have a direct understanding of the company's culture. They are attuned to the most essential services offered by the company and instinctively know when things are not working correctly. Done properly, the Help Desk staff will have strong positive relationships with the leaders and users of business departments. Those relationships are not only built by providing support but in company-wide events and daily interactions throughout the building.

A Help Desk should be the single point of contact for the company users. All requests for IT services and assistance should flow to and from the Help Desk, creating a seamless experience for the users. When a company's IT department makes a change, an internal Help Desk is better positioned to understand the customer impact and the resources needed to resolve the issue quickly. Ensuring the Help Desk is well-funded is equally important.

Negative Effects of Underfunding a Help Desk

It is critical to invest time, energy, and resources into a Help Desk to build a world-class support center. Customer support provided by the Help Desk is an expense and does not produce a direct financial benefit. Since the Help Desk is an expense, many leaders at companies will look at the Help Desk as an area to reduce costs. Leadership accomplishes these cost reductions by underfunding training, staffing, and process improvements at the Help Desk. They may also transition the Help Desk out of the IT department to an offshore service company. In the short run, a company may save money. However, in doing so, there could be long-term negative effects.

Underfunding a Help Desk could lead to poor customer satisfaction, inefficient handling of requests, and shifting issue resolution to higher cost engineers and developers. Additional effects of underfunding a Help Desk could lead to lower FCR and problems retaining staff. Naturally, providing adequate funding will avoid some of these issues. However, just giving funding without targeting the resources can lead to waste and inefficiencies.

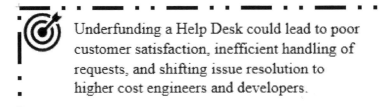

Help Desk Improvement

Throughout this book, we will discuss ways to improve the Help Desk. Our improvement efforts will focus on people, processes, and technology to combat redundancies, ad hoc efforts, and poor customer service. Our goal is to reduce or eliminate customer service delays, demoralizing employee activities, and stagnant productivity.

Managers that have implemented Help Desk improvement projects find that they are better able to avoid wasteful activities, increase operational support efficiency, and improve the overall customer experience.

Target improvement resources

Where should resources be targeted to avoid waste and inefficiencies? Most managers think of implementing new applications, hardware, or head count. I disagree. Adding new applications, hardware, and head count may increase your production support output, but it will not fix underlying problems. Your primary improvement effort focus should start with the foundation of the Help Desk. This means the core services and processes should be reviewed, documented, analyzed, and fixed where needed. This is done with a Help Desk maturity assessment. The assessment will create a detailed maturity baseline of the current state of the Help Desk. Once you have a good Help Desk maturity baseline, you can then roadmap your improvement projects. The roadmap of improvement projects will be based on actual needs instead of perceived wants. The only catch is a really good maturity assessment will also require resources to complete it.

Determine how you will fund Help Desk improvement projects

We established that not adequately funding the Help Desk is not in the company's long-term customer service interest. Maintaining or increasing Help Desk funding will better allow you to perform a maturity assessment. Once an assessment has been completed, you can create a plan to implement Help Desk improvement projects. Throughout this book, we will discuss these specific Help Desk improvement projects. Implementing these Help Desk improvement projects most likely will lead to significant improvement in efficiency, productivity, and customer satisfaction. However, as with every company, resources are not unlimited. Help Desk management will need to determine how to fund the Help Desk improvement projects.

So, when I say Help Desk improvement project funding, what do I mean? Improvement projects can be resource-intensive. Below are common activities associated with improvement projects.

Activities associated with Help Desk improvement projects

- Perform a maturity assessment of the current state and maturity of your Help Desk. Being aware that an assessment includes input from the internal team members, stakeholders, leadership, and customers, will result in more accurate and detailed results.
- Analyze assessment results by comparing current performance versus the desired industry-standard performance level.
- Identify current state strengths and weaknesses of each of your Help Desk's core areas.
- Design future state processes to correct the areas of weaknesses. Ensure you obtain input about the future state design from internal team members, stakeholders, leadership, and customers.
- Documenting the people, funding, and technology items needed to implement the future state processes.
- Obtain approval to use company resources for the improvement project.
- Execute contracts for contractors, vendors, and technology hardware and software.
- Implement the future state process.
- Train the resources that will use in the future state process.

- Communicate and educate the customers about the new process.
- Decommission the legacy process, including applicable licenses, equipment, software, and contracts.

As you can see, there are a lot of activities associated with implementing new improvement projects. Each of these activities has a cost of resource time, hardware, software, and even the opportunity cost of deferring completing other improvement projects. Also, depending on the assessment results, you may have a significant number of weaknesses identified that need to be improved. Creating an improvement roadmap based on the highest priority projects first is a good idea.

Three funding pathways

A common trait of a Help Desk is that it always seems busy. Resources have a backlog of calls waiting and tickets pending. So how do you obtain and fund the resources needed to design and implement improvement projects? There are three main options to obtain and fund resources to implement Help Desk improvement projects.

1. Obtain new additional funding.
2. Reduce expenses and use savings
3. Utilize current resources

Most Help Desk managers will leverage a combination of the three main options to fund Help Desk improvement projects. They may request partial funding, reduce some operational expenses, and reprioritize resources to work on the new improvement projects. Let us expand on each of these ways to understand them.

Funding Option 1 – Obtain new additional funding.

The improvement projects identified in this book have significant benefits. Once implemented, you may improve customer satisfaction, reduce resource consumption, and ultimately save money. You can use these projected benefits to justify your improvement projects. The vehicle typically used at a company to seek approval for project funding is a business case. A business case is a structured document that identifies an issue, outlines the proposed solution for the issue, and then outlines details for implementing the solution. These details include cost, effort, timeline, and other important details.

Experienced Help Desk managers have become very adept at creating business cases to justify projects. Being experienced in creating a business case does not mean the request will be approved. However, the better the business case, the more likely it will be approved.

Creating a Business Case

To create a business case for your Help Desk improvement project, you can follow these high-level steps.

1. **Identify the issue.** After performing a maturity assessment, you may discover your Help Desk has multiple core areas with issues that need improvement. After analyzing your issues, you should focus on one specific top priority issue for the business case. Examples of issues typically found at a Help Desk include poor First Contact Resolution (FCR) percentage, excessive call volume, or too high the average cost per ticket. The details of an identified issue should include current performance, ideal performance improvement target based on industry-standard peers, and the benefit to the company if the issue is improved. Document all this information into your business case to tell the reviewer what the issue is and why approval for this project is needed.

2. **Develop a shortlist of solution options** – So you settled on your top priority issue to fix. Now it is time to make a list of all the potential solutions that can resolve the selected issue. This list of potential solutions is what you need the money for to improve the issue identified. The solution list could include items such as purchasing a tool, customizing your current ticketing application, or hiring specialized staff to make specific improvements. Creating a shortlist of solution options assumes there is more than one way to improve the identified issue. If there is only one viable solution, then step 3 will be easy.
3. **Evaluate the solution options and select one** – Once you identify a short list of solutions for the issue, you want to select the best one. The selection process could include meeting with application vendors, setting up a test lab, or meeting with consultants. Selecting the best solution will be based on the criteria that make sense for your Help Desk. The criteria could include the ease of implementation, overall cost, and potential benefit. Once you select the preferred solution, you still want to document the top three applicable solutions in a business case. Informing the business case audience about the other solution options is important. It provides background on how the preferred solution compares to the other solution options. Thus, you will establish the context of why the preferred solution was selected.
4. **Create an implementation strategy** Once you have identified the preferred solution for the issue, you will want to create an implementation strategy. An implementation strategy is a critical part of the business case. While it does not have to be extremely detailed, it should give the approvers a sense of the time and resources that will be needed to implement the solution. The implementation strategy will identify high-level timelines, resources needed, realistic benefits, and potential

risks. If there are potential risks to implementing the solution proposed by the business case, then you should provide risk mitigation options that could be used should the risk occur.
5. **Cost/Benefit Financial Analysis** – A critical section of a business case is the financial data. You will want to explain in detail the net benefits of the improvement project and justify the expenditure. This includes identifying the tangible and intangible costs and benefits of the project. The financial data should be detailed enough to satisfy the financially focused members of the audience.
6. **Summarize your recommendation** – Probably the most important section is the business case is the executive summary section. If the approvers read nothing else, you want them to read the executive summary. This executive summary is placed at the beginning of the business case. An executive summary typically is about one page in length to sell your project. Most people write the executive summary after all the other sections of the business case have been written. The benefit to writing the summary last is you take specific information developed for each of the other sections and use it to create the one-page summary. Then if the audience has questions about any information presented in the summary, the other sections can provide the detailed context.

Funding Option 2 – Reduce expenses and use savings

If your business case is not approved, you may still be able to find the funding for your improvement project. Budgets have buckets and line items. Money is approved and allocated annually for each specific activity. In most cases, money cannot be moved around between line items without proper approval. However, you may be able to negotiate approval of a plan to implement an aggressive reduction of expenses and reallocate unused savings to the improvement project. This would keep your budget flat and allow you to proceed with the new improvement project. So, where can you find these reductions in expenses?

You may be able to reduce expenses by revisiting your current contracted services. A good place to start is to contact your vendor for each of the following services if they have been outsourced.

Contracts to renegotiate for savings

- Printing and scanning services
- Document shredding services
- Data archival services
- Computer leasing and disposal services
- Contractor labor rates
- Ticketing application licensing – pooled verses named

Vendors may offer discounts if you just ask. For example, just think of home Internet, cable, and phone services. Rates for these services seem to increase annually. Many customers have bills for these services on auto payment plans and just pay whatever amount they are billed. A modification to the services and the amount billed do not occur until the user of the service renegotiates. You may even threaten to change your service provider to a competing provider. The vendor services your Help Desk consume are no different.

Funding Option 3 – Utilize current resources

One trait of a Help Desk is the work intake can vary by day and even the time of day. Workforce management can be very complex and never perfect. The utilization of a Help Desk agent is never 100%. The volume of work on Monday mornings can be quite different than the volume of work on a Friday afternoon. Since the utilization time of the Help Desk agents can fluctuate greatly, they may have available time to work on the improvement project.

A cost-effective way of implementing an improvement project is to utilize existing resources during slow work periods. After each improvement project you implement, you will start realizing process improvements and efficiency gains. In turn, the Help Desk agents may have more time available to implement more improvement projects. You may also find that you can fully dedicate a resource or two towards creating a core improvement project team.

Where to Invest Resources

At this point, let us assume you have an idea of how you will secure resources to implement Help Desk improvement projects. You may plan to secure the resources of time and money by getting a business case approved. Maybe you plan on cutting expenses and are going to use the saving to fund the improvement projects. Perhaps your direct reports have some available work time to focus on an improvement project. Whatever the funding method you plan on using, you should decide what improvement project you want to implement. Remember, resources are finite, so your first improvement project should be wisely selected.

To help you to decide, we will discuss some of the most frequently implemented improvement projects Help Desk managers have undertaken. This information will be helpful for the business case we previously discussed. Avoid starting with the most complex issue to fix. At the beginning of your improvement effort, you will want to show a quick win. Pick a project that will have a significant benefit but is achievable in a reasonable amount of time. I have assembled a summary of the most frequently implemented improvement projects below. These project ideas are grouped by Help Desk people, process, and technology. These improvement project ideas are covered extensively in later chapters of this book.

People Focused Improvement Projects

Selecting a people-focused improvement project may be a wise choice. Your Help Desk agents are the foundational element to be able to provide great customer service. Every time a customer calls the support line, it is the Help Desk agent that has the first interaction. To exceed customers' expectations, it is important that the first customer interaction be pleasant, positive, and productive. To achieve this level of customer service it is not just about hiring good people. It is about creating a positive culture, great agent support tools, and mature processes.

When looking at the budget, Help Desk staffing is always the largest line item. Some leaders try to reduce staffing costs by reducing the headcount of agents available. These leaders think the remaining agents will become more efficient because, well, someone will have to answer the next call. This is not a good way to improve efficiency and reduce costs. When you have fewer agents handling the same amount of calls, the caller will experience an increased call queue wait time on hold waiting for the next available agent. Extended wait time in a call queue is one of the Help Desk industry's most frequent customer complaints. Reducing the number of available agents will also place a bigger burden on the agents who are working. Forcing agents to handle more calls and have shorter downtime between calls without giving them new productivity tools will lead to problems. This will lead to burnout and stress. It will also lead to poor customer service.

In this book, I focus on the cost efficiency of the staffing budget through increasing productivity using industry-standard processes and tools. Investing time, money, and resources in your people will pay big dividends in the short and long term.

Improvement project idea #1 – Implement an Employee Training and Development Program – A good Help Desk improvement project is to create or upgrade your agent training and development program. Providing training to agents means they are not on the phones providing customer support. Companies that view training as an unnecessary expense may want to reconsider. Providing structured training is crucial. Providing agents training will increase their knowledge and efficiency. Increasing the agent's knowledge will improve the first contact resolution (FCR). An increase in FCR means more issues will be resolved during the initial call with the front-line Help Desk agents. A high FCR percentage will significantly reduce the support volume of escalated issues to more expensive resources such as engineers and application developers. A Help Desk agent who receives more training has a higher probability of resolving issues quicker. When issues are resolved quicker, the agent's average call handle time is reduced. By reducing handle time, agents become more efficient and can handle more calls.

The frequency and content of the training are also very important. By providing training on a reoccurring basis, such as quarterly or annually, the curriculum will be reinforced through repetition. Knowledge retention will be increased with repeated training. The content of the training should be based on actual support issues. For example, provide training on how to resolve specific issues with a low FCR rate. It is also helpful to have on-demand or just-in-time training. An example of this is if a new IT service is being rolled out. The training can be delivered by written, video, or computer-based guides for everyone to review quickly.

A well-thought-out Help Desk agent training program is vital for success. A training program will increase the efficiency and execution of your current processes. A good training program will also be invaluable when you implement the new high-efficiency processes I will cover throughout this book. A Help Desk agent training program is so important that I dedicate an entire chapter to creating and implementing one.

For more detailed information, read: Chapter 10, Implementing an Employee Training and Development Program

Improvement project idea #2 – Create an incentive program. Rewarding good behavior leads to positive results. Providing recognition to agents that achieve specific goals can lead to high performance. The incentives offered could be monetary bonuses, but there are other ways to recognize good work. People thrive when they are officially recognized for their work. There are so many ways to recognize good work officially. One way is to give an employee a certificate of achievement. Presenting the achievement certificate during a team meeting will defiantly have an impact on the employee and their peers. Another way to recognize an employee for good work is to invite the employee to lunch with leadership. This will give the employee an opportunity to share their thoughts with leadership. Feedback from employees attending a leadership lunch is almost always positive. Some companies recognize good behavior with an employee of the month program, handwritten thank you note, or company marketing items.

Improvement project idea #3 – Create a Help Desk career path program – One of the biggest complaints of Help Desk agents is they have a dead-end job. They do not have opportunities to advance without transferring to another team in IT. It is important to support the growth of an employee working at the Help Desk by providing career path opportunities. Funding a career path structure at the Help Desk will improve the retention of your most valuable employees. The best place to have a discussion with your employees about their career path plans is to discuss this topic in a 1:1 meeting. There are many ways to offer rewarding career path options. In general, the career path track options for Help Desk agents are the management track, tiered level support track, a specialist role track, and of course, a steady eddy track.

Career Path Management Track – While staff at the Help Desk have an IT technical background, some of the staff would like to be on a management track for their career path. Developing internal resources to become a supervisor or manager can lead to a remarkably high-performing team. Some of the best leaders in the industry today started out at entry-level positions and worked their way up the ladder through a management track. Companies also find that supervisors and managers that have been internally promoted may be more loyal and may have better retention rates. By mentoring, coaching, and offering leadership training, the next leader can be developed internally.

Career Path Tiered Level Support Track – It is important to have a career path for the technical track. It is also economically beneficial to allow your least costly resources to handle most of the issues at the first level. With a tiered support structure, your first-level Help Desk agents handle the bulk of the customer contacts and resolve about 70% to 80% of the issues. Many of the customer contacts will report issues that may be repetitive. Your first-level agents will become very skilled at solving these issues quickly. As your Help Desk agents gain experience, knowledge, and skills by handling these issues, they will seek additional career challenges. This is the time you want to reward great employees and minimize attrition. A first-level Help Desk agent can be promoted to the second level. As second-level Help Desk agents, they will take on more complex issues escalated from the first-level agents. They also can be assigned to complete special projects. Not only will they be rewarded with a larger compensation, but they can develop their skill to an advanced level.

Career Path Specialist Role Track – The Help Desk has many administrative and technical duties beyond a generalist answering first-level calls. While there is also a need for a more advanced second level, there are opportunities to create full-time specialist roles. These specialist roles include primary responsibilities of managing the knowledgebase, administrating the ticketing tool, maintaining the telecom system, workforce management, major incident management, and other specific subject matter experts. Creating a specialist role for some or all these duties can lead to excellent performance and staff development. It also allows better staff-level management during high and low call volume periods. For example, a knowledgebase specialist can also log into the queue and handle overflow calls during peak time and then go back to their primary role during slow periods.

Career Path Steady Eddy – A percentage of your Help Desk agents may want a career path of just being a Help Desk agent. They may not be interested in becoming a manager, senior agent, or specialist. They just want to provide initial first-level support. That's ok. Every Help Desk needs a good base of steady eddies. Many people I have managed just want a job that is not stress-filled and likes to provide repeatable support solutions.

I outline detailed information in a later chapter-specific step on how to create an effective Help Desk career path program.

Process Focused Improvement Projects

Investing in process improvements will always pay big dividends. Having well-vetted structured processes will make the Help Desk more efficient in handling reoccurring situations and will help reduce wasted resources. When processes are repeatable, the Help Desk will increase its maturity level and efficiency. Higher volume support issues can be targeted, and the best resolution steps can be implemented. By continually reviewing and improving support processes, issues can be quickly handled and possibly reduced from occurring. To mature your Help Desk as compared to industry standards, you must have structured and repeatable processes.

Improvement project idea #4 – Perform a maturity assessment – Even though I recommend performing a maturing assessment prior to initiating improvement projects, I also listed a maturity assessment as an improvement project. Worldwide there are thousands of Help Desks doing the same work daily as your Help Desk does. There are also many companies that study those processes and determine what works well and what needs improvement. To quickly understand your Help Desk gaps, consider having a maturity assessment completed. A maturity assessment is where key stakeholders, customers, leaders, and agents will provide information about Help Desk roles, processes, technology, and the organizational structure. The final assessment report will outline the maturity level of your Help Desk compared to the industry-standard best practices. In the details of the final report, each focus area will have a specific maturity level identified. Within each focus area, gaps will be identified, and recommendations for improvements will be offered. Overall, the maturity assessment will provide a good roadmap for you to determine which improvement projects you should tackle first.

For more detailed information, read: Chapter 2, Perform a Maturity Assessment.

Improvement project idea #5 – Implement a quality assurance audit program – The only way you truly know if your staff is treating your customers properly and following all the procedures is to audit their work performance. Auditing agent performance and compliance with procedures can be accomplished by implementing an agent quality assurance audit program. This program entails listening to the agent's interaction with the customer and reviewing the support ticket documentation. The reviewer will grade the agent's call and ticket data using a standardized scorecard. Over a period, the data can paint a picture of the agent's individual performance and how they stand compared to the team's performance. Auditing provides useful information for incentive programs, annual employee performance reviews, identifying negative trends and identifying inappropriate behavior. It is critical that Help Desk management ensure agents are providing high-quality customer service. Establishing a quality assurance audit program is a recommended way to do that.

Improvement project idea #6 – Increase First Contact Resolution (FCR) – First contact resolution (FCR) is the percent of customer contact incidents that are solved by the Help Desk in the initial customer interaction without interruption divided by the total number of customer contacts.

Example FCR
Customer contacts incidents resolved: 17
Total customer contacts: 25

FCR = 17 / 25 = 0.68
FCR% = 0.68 * 100 = 68%

FCR is one of the most important Help Desk performance measurements. FCR directly ties into staffing, cost, and customer satisfaction. If your Help Desk's FCR percentage is low, ticket escalations to the 2nd level or engineers will be high. More engineers will be needed to handle the high volume of ticket escalations properly. Escalation engineers typically will have pay rates higher than frontline Help Desk agents. This means the cost per ticket handled until resolved will be higher. Also, since the customer's issue is not resolved at first contact, the customer's satisfaction level will decrease. Learn how to measure, control, and improve your team's FCR rate.

Improvement project idea #7 – Implement Performance Reporting – For some job types, managers must rely on subjective data to measure team and individual performance levels. Basically, these managers base the performance reviews on how they feel the employee is performing. This is not the case for Help Desk agents. The activities a Help Desk agent performs are objective and can be measured. There are specific industry-standard Help Desk key performance indicators (KPI) used to understand how the agent and the team are performing. This means a manager of Help Desk agents can review performance with quantifiable data.

A worthy improvement project is setting up processes to capture accurate performance data. Once you have accurate performance data, then you can compare them to industry standards. In addition, this performance data can be used as a performance measurement to gauge how effective your other improvement projects are.

Improvement project idea #8 – Create a Social Media Strategy – Now that social media has matured, it is a large part of your customer's time. Customers now have the expectation that they can use social media contact channels to obtain technical support. Customers want to leverage social media to ask technical questions, complain about products or services, and report outages or service interruptions. If a Help Desk is unable to funnel these customer contacts into their support system, then the response to these customer contacts will be inadequate. A great Help Desk improvement project is to create a robust social media process.

The Help Desk ticketing application needs to be social media aware. Corporate and Help Desk social media accounts can be linked to the ticketing application. Tickets can automatically be created based on configurable criteria. For some Help Desks, this could be a boost for customer support. For example, if a customer is discussing your company's product on social media, an automated search can track that interaction and create a support ticket for immediate follow-up. Understand how Help Desk social media strategies can be used to monitor and respond more effectively to your customers.

For more detailed information, read: Chapter XX, Create social media strategies.

Improvement project idea #9 – Leverage Help Desk Ticket Classification – The human brain does not respond well to hundreds or thousands of random data points. People and processes are more efficient when random data is arranged into similar groups. Grouped or categorized data can be more easily reviewed, analyzed, and processed compared to a large block of random data. This is why Help Desks can become more efficient when they have an effective ticket classification scheme.

Every Help Desk needs a ticket classification scheme to properly handle the customer's issues when they contact the Help Desk for support. Applying proper ticket classification immediately when a Help Desk ticket is created enables the Help Desk Agent to leverage more advanced resolution enabling tools. Ticket classification is needed to make enterprise performance reporting more accurate and meaningful. Consider an improvement project implementing ticket classification to improve escalations, resolution, and reporting of Help Desk tickets.

Improvement project idea #10 – Design a Call Volume Management Strategy – Some people think inbound call volume to the Help Desk is unpredictable. This is not accurate. A wise Help Desk manager will study their inbound call volume patterns. Once you understand the fundamentals of inbound call volume, you can implement processes and controls to manage them better. An incredible improvement project is to implement processes and controls to manage Help Desk call volume.

With this improvement project, you will understand what drives your call volume and its patterns. You will evaluate and implement processes and tools to control, shape, and reduce the call volumes to manageable flows. Once implemented, you will realize tangible benefits to managing call volumes. These benefits include reduced support costs, better staffing models, and improved customer satisfaction.

Improvement project idea #11 – Chapter XX: Implement a Shift-Left Support Strategy – Understand how a shift-left customer support strategy can reduce costs, improve resolution times, and empower your customers. Shift-left is based on the customer on the far left and SME engineers on the far right. I will guide you in the process of shifting customer support closer to the customer. For example, some types of incident tickets currently handled by SME engineers are moved to the Help Desk. Some types of requests handled by the Help Desk are moved to customer self-service offerings.

Technology Focused Improvement Projects

To support customers and the IT services they consume, a Help Desk needs solid applications that are integrated. Good technology systems will increase the efficiency of the Help Desk agent. They also can provide detailed enterprise support data for business analytics.

However, new technology tools can be expensive. To understand the cost of new technology, you need to calculate the total cost of ownership. The total cost of ownership is not just the purchase cost of new technology. In addition to the purchase cost, there are many additional costs that add up to the total cost of ownership. Examples of this additional cost are the installation, licensing, maintenance, and upgrades you will incur over the life of the technology use.

Improvement project idea #12 – Supercharge your Ticketing Application – The foundation of all Help Desks is the ticketing application. All Help Desks need a way to capture the customer support information, be able to escalate issues and prioritize their workload. A basic ticketing application will allow you to do these things. Are you fully leveraging all the functionality of your current ticketing application? Is your current ticket application meeting your current needs?

Today's feature-rich and integrated application will allow your team to do so much more. Some of these features are part of the base ticketing application. Other features may require an additional licensing cost to unlock the functionality. Some of the most popular additional features of a ticketing application are a service catalog, knowledgebase, CTI integration, and social media connections.

For more detailed information, read: Chapter XX Create a Unified Ticketing Platform.

Improvement project idea #13 – Offer your Customers a Service Catalog – If your Help Desk already has some solid processes in place, you may want to consider a more advanced improvement project. Implementing a service catalog can take your service request fulfillment processes to the next level. A service catalog is a list of all IT services available to users to request or order. The service catalog will provide basic information about the service offered, such as name, description, and how to order the service. Service catalogs can be designed to generate a provisioning request ticket in the ticketing application. A system of automated workflow rules can drive the process of request approval and shepherd it through the provisioning process.

Improvement project idea #14 – Give your Knowledgebase some Wisdom – A knowledgebase system integrated into your ticketing application is a must. Making upgrades to your knowledge base is an important improvement project you can undertake. A robust knowledge base system can reduce the time for an agent to find the support knowledge they need while assisting a customer on the phone. This reduces call handle time and allows agents to answer the next call in queue quicker. Usually, this is accomplished by providing the most relevant knowledge base solutions to a Help Desk agent when they enter the ticket category. Knowledgebase articles can also be presented based on a keyword search or by using a decision tree script. A knowledge base can also be presented to users via a self-service portal.

Improvement project idea #15 – Upgrade your Computer and Telephone Integration (CTI) – The two basic systems all Help Desk agents use are a computer and a telephone. CTI is the term used for the functionality to integrate the computer and telephone to work together. An integrated ticketing and phone system allow customer information and previous history to be displayed within the application when a call is answered. This displaying of the customer information on a Help Desk agent's computer screen is called a screen pop. A screen pop will save a lot of time and reduce human error as compared to a Help Desk agent manually searching for a customer's records.

Improvement project idea #16 – Implement Remote Desktop Control – Whether the Help Desk agent's customer is on a different floor or in a different state, using a remote desktop control application is almost a must. Using a remote support application allows the Help Desk agent to see the video out on the monitor while controlling the mouse and keyboard. Prior to Help Desks using a remote support application, the Help Desk agent had to verbally explain to the user what to type and click to resolve an issue. The user had to perform these actions as directed and then try to explain what the displayed result of that action was. This is very confusing and time-consuming. Remote support applications now support working on laptops, desktops, and mobile devices. In addition, all support activities provided can be recorded and stored to be used in the future for auditing and training purposes.

Implementing Help Desk Improvement Projects Worksheet

The following are general overview steps for selecting, obtaining approval, and implementing Help Desk improvement projects.

Step 1 – Take the Help Desk maturity assessment

Perform a maturity assessment of the current state and maturity of your Help Desk. Visit the Help Desk Management book's companion resource website and complete the Help Desk maturity assessment. To try the IT Help Desk Maturity Assessment, click the following link.

https://buildahelpdesk.com/help-desk-maturity-assessment-guide/

Step 2 – Analyze the maturity assessment results.

Analyze the maturity assessment results by comparing each of the core area maturity level scores you received to the desired industry-standard performance level of level 4 or 5. To learn more about mature processes for each of the core areas, visit one or all the following resources.

- Read specific chapters of this Help Desk Management book.
- Information and blog posts on the book's companion resource site https://buildahelpdesk.com
- Subscribe to the Help Desk Management YouTube channel Help Desk Management - YouTube

Step 3 - Design a future state process

In this step, you want to design a future state process for systems and services that make up the core areas that you scored low in the maturity assessment. In the chapter, we provided several improvement project recommendations. Ensure you obtain input about the future state design from internal team members, stakeholders, leadership, and customers.

Step 4 - Identify the resources needed
Documenting the people, funding, and technology items needed to design, build, and implement the future state processes. This information will assist you in determining project funding and a timeline to build a business case or budget request.

Step 5 - Obtain improvement project approval
Obtain approval to use company resources for the improvement project. Some improvement projects are smaller in scale. It might mean you already have the resources and authority to start improving the process. Other projects may require significant time and money. For these project requests, follow your company's approval process.

Step 6 - Initiate the improvement project
Execute contracts for contractors, vendors, and technology hardware and software.

Step 7 - Complete the project
Implement the future state process.

Step 8 - Train your staff
Train the resources that will be using the future state process.

Step 9 Customer communications
Communicate and educate the customers about the new process.

Step 10 - Decommission the legacy process -
Decommission the legacy process, including applicable licenses, equipment, software, and contracts.

Chapter 4:

Create a Mission Statement

Chapter Objectives

- Identify the benefits of a mission statement.
- Define who the audience is for your mission statement.
- Create a mission statement.

Many companies and department leaders will overlook creating and promoting a mission statement. This chapter will try to convince you of the importance of a mission statement. To create an effective department mission statement, you must first understand the purpose. A mission statement defines the reason your company exists, what it does, and how it does it. It may include aspects of operations, highlight products or services, and specifics about unique customers. You may also see mission statements that include company values and what makes the company better than the competition. The company mission statement reflects every facet of the business and all the departments. For these reasons, a mission statement is the cornerstone of your company by communicating its purpose. The mission statement is generally short but powerful.

Corporate Mission Statement

Almost every company nowadays has a mission statement for the entire company. A company is made up of many different departments, such as finance, human resources, sales, and others. Since the corporate mission statement covers all departments, resources, products, and services, it has to be high level and inclusive. The IT department with the Help Desk as part of it may be only a small portion of the company. Therefore, you should consider creating a department or team mission statement.

Departmental Mission Statement

Many Information Technology departments, including Help Desk teams, will define a department-level mission statement. A department-level mission statement should not conflict with the company-level statement but supplement it. Your department's mission statement is the foundation from which your organizational chart, processes, attitude, and customer interaction are built. It assists you in evaluating your current state and goals. Mission statements will unify the department in a strategic direction. Take ownership and control of your most important statement.

Benefits of a Mission Statement

It is surprising with all the information about mission statements available that some companies and departments choose not to have one. In other instances, some companies and departments may have a mission statement, but it is significantly dated. Having a focused and up-to-date mission statement will assist in planning and executing department activities. Here are some of the benefits of a mission statement.

Provides a Department Compass – Earlier, we said a mission statement states our values, how we do our work, and where we aspire to be. A mission statement can be a lodestar to inspire and guide the direction of your department, especially when tough decisions need to be made. People refer to a mission statement as a compass. A compass will constantly display the direction you are traveling. Like using a compass, a mission statement will allow you to periodically validate you are going in the correct direction towards your goal. If you happen to be off course, you can make adjustments to get back on track.

Formal Commitment to Goals – A mission statement is a documented affirmation by leadership and staff on the department's core beliefs, values, and how the department will handle customers. This affirmation is very important. If leadership is not on board with the mission statement, then the effort will fail. If the staff does not embrace the mission statement, there will be little progress towards the aspirational goals stated in it. That is why it must be a formal and public agreement to follow the mission statement completely. Everyone must know the entire department is on board and being true to the mission statement.

Enhance Staff Integration – Have you ever worked for a company where your peers seem to be doing their own thing? In a situation like this, you may be on the same team, but so much energy is wasted arguing about how work is supposed to be done. A mission statement can reduce confusion and align staff to work together. A mission statement can build a cohesive team culture. A mission statement can reflect a department's common goal and purpose. When there is an issue, the team can come together and review the mission statement. They can review the issue together and figure out a home to overcome it. By working together, the staff will become integrated with a common purpose.

Support your Company's Brand – One of the most important things for a company from the customer's perception is its brand. The brand is the identity of the company. The brand makes a lasting impression on the customer. For a company brand to be effective, all the company's employees need to be unified in the work they do to support the brand. A mission statement will be a constant reminder of how to be true to the brand. For example, if part of your department brand is to be known for outstanding customer service, then your mission statement should reflect this in part. The entire team should be empowered to strive for 100% customer satisfaction in every interaction with the customer.

Mission Statement Audience

When creating or updating a mission statement, you really need to consider the audience. The mission statement is not created for one person or group in mind. It should be created for an audience made up of customers, employees, and investors.

Customers The lifeblood of any company is its customers. The mission statement should directly or indirectly state how customers should be valued. By setting lofty customer service goals and affirming good customer practices, your department will build a customer-friendly culture. This culture leads to rewarding work for the staff and positive business interactions for the customer.

Employees Departments are made up of people. By making a commitment to treat employees with respect, a positive environment will ultimately be achieved. This will create a productive and rewarding culture. The mission statement should inspire everyone to achieve this work environment goal.

Investors People and groups that invest in companies are looking for long-term success and a return on their money. In addition to the financial considerations, they are looking for a company with a great team. A team that can overcome challenges and that achieves the goals they set. Creating and following a mission statement will affirm the value of your company as a worthy investment.

Mission Statement Building Worksheet

We discussed what a mission statement is. We explained that a department's mission statement should clearly and precisely be focused on what your Help Desk is all about and related to the customer support your team provides. The mission statement will bring the strategic focus of underlining the goals and objectives of your team based on company values. We also discuss the benefits of a mission statement. Now it's time to build your department's mission statement.

Objectives

When building your department's mission statement, your goal is to meet the following three objectives.

Create a department mission statement that incorporates your company's goals, objectives, and values.

Integrate the mission statement into your department's culture and processes.

Communicate your mission statement to your customers in both a communication plan and daily support interaction.

Creating a department mission statement

This chapter assumes you are focused on departmental improvements and may have a company-wide mission statement in place. The same principles discussed in this chapter for department-level mission statements are the same for company-wide statements. If you do not have a company-wide mission statement to start with, that is ok. Proceed with your department's mission statement creation with a clean slate. To create a departmental mission statement, you first should completely understand what the goals and objectives of the company you work for are. It is important to make sure the new department's mission statement aligns and does not conflict with the corporate mission statement. By reflecting on the corporate mission statement, determine what your department does to help the company meet those goals and objectives. The mission statement should be written from the customer's perspective, be very specific, and it should fit with the vision for the business. The mission statement should answer the following mission statement building questions:

Step 1 – Mission Statement Building Questions

Part of the process of creating a mission statement is to reflect on the below questions and document your answers.

What do we do?
How do we do it?
For whom do we do it?
What sets us apart from our competitors?
How will you use your resources to reach your goals?
What words best describe your team, service, and customers?

This exercise is not just for the department leader to complete. Creating a mission statement is a department-wide effort. It is important to assemble many voices from your department to gather input by answering these questions. What is the best way to get input from a good cross representation of voices from your department? We suggest assembling a project team and holding a focus group.

Step 2 – Assemble the Project Team

It's important to assemble the core mission statement project team members before proceeding. There are specific resources you will need to avoid becoming overwhelmed with tasks.

Project leader – The person in charge of the project who will, with input, create the scope, define tasks, and keep everyone on track.

Technical Writer – Holding a focus group and creating a mission statement requires a person with good documentation skills.

Meeting Facilitator – Running a lively focus group is not for everyone. Having someone trained or at least familiar with how to run one effectively will improve the input. Ideally, the facilitator will have a technical writer take notes and possibly videotape the session.

Communication resource – While communication is important for the entire project, it is especially important during the implementation stage. A communication resource will ensure the stakeholders, project team, and other groups are informed of the status.

Customer / Business liaison – This is a person who can assist with identifying focus group participants, evaluating mission statement drafts, and assisting with the implementation.

Step 3 – Prepare Focus Group Meetings

In this section, we will discuss what the project team will need to do to prepare for the mission statement focus group meetings.

Create a focus group agenda

State the purpose of the focus group, which is to gather input from the group to build an effective mission statement. Remember, the purpose of a focus group is to focus on this single topic.

To establish your objectives for the focus group meeting, start building your agenda by using the six-mission statement building questions. These questions will help you stay focused and gather good information.

Identify who you want to invite to the focus group meeting. You should have a good cross representation of staff, leaders, customers, and business partners. If you identify more than ten people to invite, consider creating multiple focus groups.

If you do have enough participants to create two or more focus groups, then make one a control group. A control group is the specific target group, which is the Help Desk. The second group would be the one with a good balance across the company. This will allow you to compare answers from internal to external groups.

Build into the agenda enough time for participant discussion. Remember, this is not a presentation but a forum to get specific input from the group.

Gather the focus group meeting materials.

Reserve a room large enough to host the meeting.
Whiteboard or presentation easel.
Markers, pens, and pencils.
Large post-it notes cards.
Large wallpaper so you can attach the post-it notes.
Name tags and table tents.
Tape.

Arrange the room

It is important the room is set up to maximize participation in the focus group. Here are some general ideas on how to arrange the room.

Room setup – Arrange the tables and chairs in a square, U shape, or circle. The idea is to have people facing each other to spur discussion and collaboration.

Presentation – Please put the whiteboard or presentation easel in a spot where everyone can see it.

Tools – Place the following supplies in each spot.

Handouts – Print out the agenda, name tent, pens, markers, paper, and post-it note cards.

Step 4 – Hold Focus Group Meetings

Now that you have assembled the project team, have an agenda, have gathered the materials, and set up the room, it's time to run the focus group meeting. This section will discuss how to run a focus group and how to obtain the output you need.

Meeting Start Tips

Attendance – Have all participants sign in to keep a record of who attended.

Names – Have the participants put their name on a table tent and place it in front of them.

Greeting – Acknowledge that people are busy and thank them for attending.

Overview – Set the stage for the group. Describe the project and what you hope to gain from the group. In this case, we want input from the focus group about the Help Desk.

Agenda – Review the agenda of the meeting. Go over how it will proceed and how the members can participate.

During the Meeting Tips

Neutrality – As a moderator, remain impartial and neutral. Don't provide positive or negative feedback. Just thank them for sharing.

Active listening – Validate long-winded or unfocused comments by summarizing what they said. To confirm what member state, start by saying, "here is what I understood you said."

Different viewpoints – Remember, there is no right answer. You are trying to gather their perspective even if their feedback is contrary to your understanding.

Equal time – Make sure all members get a chance to be heard and express their opinion. For shy participants, prompt them with follow-up questions to elicit more information.

Engage participants – Prompt members that are engaged in discussion with a specific question directed to those people.

Rephrase questions – Sometimes, people understand a question better if you restate it in a different way.

Wrapping Up the Meeting Tips

Summarize next steps – Prior to the meeting ending, provide the group an overview of the project status and what are the next tasks.

Be thankful – Thank everyone for participating.

Contact information – Provide everyone a way to contact the project team if they want to provide more information.

Personalized meeting – Offer to meet individually with any participant that would feel more comfortable providing feedback in a private setting.

Step 5 – Post Meeting tasks

Debriefing – Immediately following the focus group session, the facilitator and note-takers need to review all the focus group input received. This includes the notes taken during the meeting, written information from the participants, and thoughts from the focus group facilitators. Do not wait to hold this meeting. It is important to discuss the input while it is still fresh.

Control the input – Make sure all focus group input is documented, copied, and saved for the historical record. This includes flip charts, pictures of whiteboards, and all papers.

Organize the input – Review the input and determine if there are common themes. Start categorizing the input into similar categories. The categories should be arranged based on the questions we discussed previously.

What do we do?
How do we do it?
For whom do we do it?
What sets us apart from our competitors?
How will you use your resources to reach your goals?
What words best describe your team, service, and customers?

Step 6 – Assemble a mission statement

With the organized focus group input, you can start to formulate answers to the following questions. These answers will be in the form of a short statement of one sentence. The answers will be combined to form a mission statement paragraph. The paragraph will then be modified with keywords that will enhance the final product.

Create a short statement for each of the following questions.

Question 1 – What does your team do? (example: We provide technical support for our company's accounting software)

Question 2 – How does your team do it? (example: We handle support requests by phone and email 24/7/365)

Question 3 – For whom does your team do it? (example: We provide support to our external customers using our accounting software)

Question 4 – What sets your team apart from your competitors? (Example: We ensure 100% customer satisfaction, or we will refund your purchase.)

Question 5 – How will your team use its resources to reach your goals? (Example: Our team will respond to all calls with professionalism and use our expertise to resolve issues.)

Question 6 – What words best describe your team? Your service? Your customers?

Put the answers together to form a basic mission statement.

Example – We provide technical support for our company's accounting software by phone and email 24/7/365 to our external customers. We ensure 100% customer satisfaction, or we will refund your purchase. Our team will respond to all calls with professionalism and use our expertise to resolve issues.

Identify the positive words used by the focus group to describe your team, its service, and customers

Example – Teamwork, passionate, determined, fun, creative, outstanding, award-winning, family, loyal, globally

Add selected positive words to the basic mission statement to enhance it.

Example – We provide outstanding technical support for our company's accounting software by phone and email 24/7/365 to our loyal customers globally. We are determined to ensure 100% customer satisfaction, or we will refund your purchase. Our team will respond to all calls with professionalism and use our expertise to resolve issues.

Department ownership of the mission statement

Once you create a mission statement, you are not done. Simply communicating the mission statement once to your staff will lead to sure failure. Your entire team needs to understand and embrace your mission statement in everything they do. It must be ingrained into your culture. The staff needs to be introduced to the mission statement in a team meeting format. The statement should be discussed. All the keywords in the mission statement should be discussed in detail. Handouts should be provided, and all web pages, documents, and team areas should have the mission statement visible.

Implementing a Mission Statement

Initial rollout

Print a copy of the mission statement for every employee.

Gather your employees and review the mission statement together.

Ask employees what specifically the mission statement means to them with specific examples.

Reinforcement

Add the mission statement to the employee handbook, onboarding training guide, and other department documents.

Create a poster-size printout of the mission statement and place it in highly visible areas in the department, such as the breakroom, entryway, and workspace area.

Create card-size printouts of the mission statement to place on the employee's phone or computer monitor. This will reinforce the mission when the Help Desk agents are providing customer support.

How to communicate your new mission statement to your customer.

Rolling out your new mission statement to your customers is very important. You want your customers to know what your business is all about and how much you value providing award-winning customer support. Ensure the mission statement is prominently available for your customers to see and review. A prominent location will most likely be your Intranet or Internet home page. We suggest that your mission statement be displayed on your public-facing support page. This could be a page on the company Intranet or a self-service portal. It is also recommended that your mission statement be included in any communication from your team to your customers. This can include email notifications, published support documents, and training material.

Make it visible

Add your mission statement to your public-facing Help Desk support page.

Add your mission statement to your customer email communications, such as the support ticket open and closure emails.

Ensure your customer satisfaction surveys include questions that are based on your mission statement values.

Chapter 5:

Employee and Customer Support Structure

Chapter Objectives

- ➤ Understand employee support structures important for a Help Desk.
  - Employee's access to policies.
  - Policy training.
  - Employee acknowledgement of policies.
  - Attendance policy.
  - Scheduling Policy.
  - Security Policy.
  - Computer Use Policy.

- ➤ Understand customer support structures important for a Help Desk.
  - Customer contact channels.
  - Hours of operation.
  - Support location.
  - Supported languages.
  - Official records.

Implementing the employee and customer support structures is important for any company and department to function efficiently and fairly. The employee support structure handles human resource policy, hierarchical reporting, salary policy, benefits policy, and much more company-wide policies. There is also a more specific department-level employee support structure, which provides tactical guidance to all employees of the department and is in compliance with the corporate organizational structure. There are also many policies and procedures for customer support. In this chapter, we are focusing on the employee and customer support structure. We will discuss the most frequently used policies and procedures.

Employee support structure

Managers know that well-thought-out job-related policies are important for employees to meet or exceed expectations. Implementing fair and consistent policies related to time away, disciplinary, and grievance issues gives clear direction and creates an environment where employees are engaged and happy. It also provides managers structure on how to manage and be fair appropriately. There are many policy fundamentals you should be aware of to ensure you get the best performance from your employees and are covered legally.

Access to Policies – Similar to the corporate policies, Help Desk departmental policies must be readily accessible to the employees. Readily accessible means the policies should be stored on an internal read-only website, SharePoint page, or another electronic repository that allows access at any time. Employees should be notified where and how to be able to access the policy repository. If an employee has trouble accessing the policies, there should be a method to report this issue and a process to resolve an access issue.

Policy Training – To successfully comply with department policies, employees must understand the policies. Employees should receive initial policy training when they onboard into the department. The employee should also receive reoccurring policy training. It is common practice for employees to receive at least annual refresher training on policies. An annual review of departmental policies is critical to remind employees of the department's expectations. Many companies will create computer-based learning videos to provide this training. The benefit of computer-based training is the content is the same for all employees. Computer-based training also creates an audit trail to track completion and compliance. If computer-based training is used, there must be a process to allow the employee to ask questions and for clarifications. At the end of the training, content and acceptance agreement should be displayed to have the employee acknowledge they received the training.

Employee acknowledgment – Once the employee receives training and has all their questions answered, the employee should sign a statement agreeing to comply with the policies. Upon completion of computer-based training, employees should acknowledge that they have received the training. Having a documented acknowledgment from the employee is important if ever the employee must have a corrective action. This will eliminate the argument that the employee did not know the expectations required of them.

Specific Help Desk Policies

Attendance Policy

We all agree employees should show up for work on time for their scheduled shift, and most employees do. However, to set expectations, you need to document what steps the employees should take if they are running late, sick, or have some emergency keeping them from arriving on time. Successful Help Desk Managers know that they need a specific attendance policy that goes above and beyond the corporate attendance policy. The Help Desk staffing model is very sensitive to unplanned absences, and a well-defined attendance policy can help you maintain acceptable staffing levels. New Help Desk Agents should receive attendance policy training and a written copy on day one. The policy should be online and available for the Help Desk Agents. Your attendance policy should define what absences are. Both planned and unplanned absences should be covered. The policy should identify the steps and time frame the employee must follow to notify their supervisor they will be absent. Remember, a good attendance policy will improve workforce management, reduce customer wait time, and improve morale for the team.

Scheduling Policy

Creating a shift schedule for a 24/7/365 Help Desk can be challenging. Creating a schedule can lead to much conflict for employees and management. While there are many shifts that need to be covered, not all shifts are desirable. Most of your employees will want to work the day shift on weekdays. While most of the customers do contact the Help Desk during the weekday, dayshift, night, weekend, and overnight shifts will need coverage. A Help Desk manager will need to have a policy in place, defining how shifts will be scheduled and how to handle conflicts. This policy must be fair, and it must be communicated to the staff well in advance of implementing it to set expectations.

Master schedule – The management team will start the process by analyzing the workload and creating a master schedule with every shift defined. The needed shifts to cover the call volume can include a variety of start and end times, the number of days worked each week, and shift overlapping coverage. Once the master schedule has been completed, the next step is to identify an agent for each shift. There are many ways of doing this, and we have a few examples.

Management defined – Creating a schedule by management defining the schedule with little input is the easiest for a manager. However, this can cause the most conflict. Many agents, over time, will like to change their shifts. Once the schedule has been completed, management will post the schedule. Allowing agents the ability to trade shifts will reduce conflict.

Scheduling by seniority – Creating a schedule by seniority does have its advantages. It is very easy to identify every employee's hire date and create a shift selection order. The most senior agent will select their shift first and then continue until the least senior agent has selected their shift. Senior employees will appreciate the priority of scheduling. There are many disadvantages to creating a schedule based on seniority. Managers will give up control of which employees are working on which shift. The result could be the experienced staff are working weekday day shifts, and the least experienced people may end up working nights and weekend shifts. Also, if the Help Desk does not have a lot of turnovers, the shift schedule may not change very much.

Schedule by top 3 – Another scheduling option is to allow the staff to choose their top 3 shift options. The manager will review all the selections and put together a final shift schedule. An advantage of this process is the employee will be able to choose three shift options that they prefer. Another advantage is the Help Desk manager does have some control to create a schedule based on experience and other attributes. A disadvantage of this selection process is there will be shifts no one will choose. A process will have to be defined on how to fill these shifts.

How to fill night and weekend shifts – It will always be a challenge to fill night and weekend shifts. The best way to avoid conflict is to hire staff, specifically for these shifts. Offering a shift differential will also make staffing the nights and weekend shifts easier. A shift differential is extra pay for staff such as a percentage above their normal pay. Another way to fill nights and weekend shifts with experienced agents is by offering a career path to employees. By creating specific roles such as weekend manager or night shift team lead, you can promote agents into the night and weekend roles.

Security Policy

Help Desk personnel usually have elevated permission to reset passwords, install software, and navigate data repositories.

Administrative accounts with elevated permissions need to be secure and controlled. A security best practice is to ensure the Help Desk personnel only have the appropriate amount of elevated permissions necessary to do their job and only use elevated permissions when necessary. To enforce security controls, many companies give Help Desk agents two accounts. The first account is their day-to-day account, where they can do most of their activities that do not require an elevated level of permission. When they do need elevated permissions, they use a secondary account that has administrator rights. Typical uses of these elevated permission accounts are used when they need to work with passwords, installs, and such. Another option many companies are now using in security applications is an enterprise password management system. These systems allow the changing of passwords enterprise-wide when people change roles or leave the company. It manages temporary passwords for vendors and contractors to allow their passwords to change when needed automatically. Auditing account use is a very helpful option to know who used an account and when.

Computer Use Policy

Your company most likely already has a computer use policy. A computer use policy will define what you can and cannot do with the company's technology. If your company does not have a computer use policy or you want to define additional department guidance, then you will have to develop one. The computer use policy should cover the following at a minimum.

Notifying the employee that the computer and all the data on it is company property.

The employee is not allowed to install non-standard hardware or software.

The employee may not use the computer to harass others.

Guidance on the Internet and social media access.

Providing computer use guidance on locking and securing the computer when away from their workspace or traveling.

Providing computer use guidance on how to report misuse, inappropriate behavior, or to ask a question.

Making sure the employee knows what is expected of them is important.

Customer support structure

As with the foundation of a house, a good support structure is needed to build out your Help Desk. If you do not have a solid Help Desk support structure in place, then your Help Desk will have many unnecessary and more intense problems. The Help Desk support structure determines how customers are handled and how information flows within the Help Desk department. There are many factors, rules, and policies to consider when you design your Help Desk structure. These decisions include defining contact channels used, hours of operation, the language supported, customer base location, security practices, and many other items. The Help Desk support structure must be documented. Customers should receive regular communication on how support works and how it is performing.

Customer Contact Channels

How should the customer contact support? Customers will engage support from the Help Desk using a contact channel. A contact channel is an avenue that is available for the customer to use to initiate support from your Help Desk. Historically the primary contact channel is a phone call between the customer and the Help Desk. Phones are readily available to customers and very convenient. Phone calls offer advantages such as live interaction with the Help Desk Agent and typically a good chance for an immediate resolution to the issue.

However, there are some disadvantages to having customers report issues or request services using a phone call. Potential long call wait time during a high-volume period is a common issue. Customer dissatisfaction with the Help Desk is frequently attributed to being on hold for an extended period. Also, a phone call is one of the most expensive contact channel options since it requires a higher level of staffing.

Customers have demanded more contact channel options in addition to the traditional phone call. Help Desk management should offer the customer the ability to request support in the method they prefer. Help Desk management also realizes offering multiple contact channels will help reduce costs and improve customer satisfaction. These additional contact channels include email, web portal, chat, and social media.

For consistency, you should decide what official contact channels are available for use by your customers. Once you formally decide on what contact channels will be available, you must also ensure the customer is also aware of what is available by marketing and training. Setting expectations on how and when support will be provided is an important part of that awareness. With response time, for example, the expectation to answer a call could be seconds or minutes versus an email which could be hours or days. Many companies that offer most or all types of contact channels will state that if your issue is urgent or impacting many people, please call for assistance. In this case, they are stating to the customer that calling will provide the quickest and most reliable response time verse other contact channels.

Hours of operation

For businesses competing in a global Internet-driven economy, it is important to define your core support operations hours. If the core support hours are 24/7/365, then you must ensure you have around-the-clock coverage to handle support issues. If the core support hours are anything other than 24/7/365, then you should consider offering options for support after-hour emergency coverage. If you do offer after-hour emergency coverage, you must define what constitutes an emergency. Whatever Help Desk management decides its hours of operation are, the customer must understand it. The Help Desk web portal printed support material, service level agreements, and all communication should explicitly describe what support is available, when, and how.

Support base location

Many companies create a centralized support team, which is a locally based team to provide daytime, evening, graveyard, weekend, and holiday support coverage. Staffing all of these shifts in one location can be a challenge if the company resides in a small or medium-sized city with a small labor force pool. Some companies create a decentralized support model. Decentralized support is where support labor resides in other cities, states, or countries close to the customer base and loosely collaborates with the company headquarters. A disadvantage of a decentralized model does have inefficiencies if each support location must staff for their local contact volume. A third option is a hybrid support model. A hybrid virtual support model is where support labor from any location logs into a centralized platform for contact channels, communication, ticketing, and collaboration. The hybrid model increases the available talent pool substantially and reduces the administrative inefficiencies of multiple decentralized support locations.

Language

English is the primary corporate business language of the United States and many countries. However, this is changing with the significant rise of Spanish and other popular languages. Most companies offer customer support in multiple languages, especially if they have operations outside the United States. When contacting support by phone, customers should be presented with the option to select which language they would like to communicate with if more than one is available. If the company's operations or customer base has a significant base in a country where English Is not the primary language, many companies will have a support center in that country. By having a support center in the country, Help Desk agents will have an appropriate dialect and understand cultural norms. In a hybrid staffing model, support resources outside the United States can receive support calls with non-English selected as the communication method.

Official records

As with most business and consumer transactions, an official record of the support interaction is a must. Keeping a record of the customer request and the fulfillment of the request is necessary for compliance, auditing, and various other requirements.

Ticketing application records – The preferred option is to use a ticketing application where you can record the specific details of the interaction with the customer. Most ticketing applications allow you to create workflows to track requests from start to finish. One area receiving a lot of scrutiny is password resets. Audits frequently are focused on the process to identify the user and how those requests are fulfilled.

Call recordings – The Help Desk should keep all call recordings between the customer and Help Desk agent for an established time period. Since most corporations have record retention policies, call recording retention policies for the Help Desk should be established and compliant with the overall corporate policy. As a manager, having the ability to review the recorded interactions will allow for better training and coaching of the agent. Retaining call recordings will also establish an audit trail for policy and procedure compliance.

Other official records – You may also want to retain emails, chat interactions, and other transactions between the customer and the support person as official records. These contact channels are very popular, but the auditing and review of these can be more cumbersome compared to efficient call recording systems.

Employee and Customer Support Structure Worksheet Checklist

We discussed the basic organizational and support structure processes at the Help Desk. This worksheet is a checklist built from the last chapter. Your goal is to review the organizational and support structure processes you have in place and to determine what areas of improvement are needed.

Checkpoint 1 – Validate you have the following policies in place and active.

1. **Attendance Policy** – A document to inform employees how different types of planned and unplanned leaves will be handled.
2. **Schedule policy** – This document will outline the available shifts at your Help Desk. It should outline critical procedures such as how to request shifts and how shifts are awarded.
3. **Security policy** – The Help Desk security policy is more than the general computer and network use policy for end users. The Help Desk security policy should also cover Identity and Access Management (IAM) processes owned by the Help Desk.
4. **Customer call and ticket handling policy** – Customers have the right to be treated fairly and the same. This policy will outline those rights.

Checkpoint 2 – Validate the policies that have been reviewed by management in the last 12 months.

Checkpoint 3 – Validate a read-only accessible policy repository is in place and being used to store and display departmental policies.

Checkpoint 4 – Do you have a communication process in place to let employees know where these policies are located?

Checkpoint 5 – Do you have an active employee policy training program in place?

1. Onboarding
2. Annual training
3. Just in time training.

Checkpoint 6 – At the conclusion of employee training, do you have employees sign a statement that they understand the policies?

Checkpoint 7 – Do you have a customer information-sharing portal and share the following information?

1. Contact channels available and attributes of each.
2. The hours of operation of the Help Desk are posted.
3. An after-hour escalation process to follow when there are urgent issues.
4. Languages are available for support.

Help Desk People Section

The Help Desk is made up of people supporting customers by using technology and following procedures. While the technology and procedures are very important, many will argue that the Help Desk staff are the most critical component. Only with a highly motivated and trained staff at the Help Desk can the team deliver award-winning customer service. In the following chapters, we will discuss key topics on how to motivate and train your Help Desk staff to reach this level. We will discuss what a new manager should do to understand their team. We will then help management create effective job descriptions. After, we will discuss what meetings are needed and provide sample meeting agendas. We will discuss the best certifications your staff should have and why. Finally, we will help the Help Desk management team set up a training and development program.

Chapter 6:

Understand your team

Chapter Objectives

- Understand the team's organizational structure.
- Obtain and review employee data.
- Understand and update the supervisor to staff ratio.
- Complete the supervisor to staff ratio worksheet.

Starting a new role as manager of a team can have many challenges. One of the biggest challenges for a new manager is understanding their team. While it is important to understand the personalities of the individuals working on your team, it may be more important to understand your team in the sense of structure and processes. Every company has unique organizational structures, job descriptions, use of specialists, and staff to management ratios. If you recognize and study the efficiencies of these structures and processes, you can make informed decisions for improvements. Positive improvements will increase productivity, reduce costs, and improve the overall work-life balance.

Organizational Structure

Before you hold detailed meetings with individuals on your new Help Desk team, you really need to understand the team's organizational structure. Your first task is to obtain an organizational chart from your supervisor or the Human Resources department.

When studying the organizational chart, there are some important aspects to note. You should know how the organizational structure is defined. Your staff and the customers they support may be arranged by one of the following approaches.

Organization by functional roles

An organization that breaks employees into groups based on their knowledge and skills is called a functional organizational structure. This creates specific departments, such as marketing, engineering, and information technology. This results in a top-down approach with functional heads. The staff works together internally most of the time, with limited interaction with other functional groups. Most of the interaction between groups is handled at the group leadership level. The advantage of creating a functional organizational structure is that it enables employees to specialize and become experts in job roles. Having specialists work on the same activity can lead to high levels of efficiency and work quality. There also is a clear reporting structure since an employee has one direct manager. However, there are disadvantages to organizing by functional roles. Teams can become too insulated from other departments. Due to this limited interaction with other groups, problems can arise in working with other departments.

Organization by the divisional structure

When a self-sufficient team is organized to focus on a single location, market, service, or product, it can be referred to as a divisional organizational structure. An example of this is when automobile companies have an autonomous organizational structure for certain corporate brands and models of cars. The advantage of a divisional structure is that decisions can be made based on the divisional needs for their location, market, service, or product. The division becomes more responsive to its customer's needs. The disadvantage of a divisional structure is that there are duplicate functions needed for each division. Each division may have its own marketing, engineering, and information technology department. This leads to a larger staff size than you would see in an organization grouped functionally.

Organization by the matrix structure

The matrix organizational structure is very different than organizing by functional or divisional structure. In the matrix organizational structure, an employee could report to a manager based on their function. They could also report to another manager based on the product or service line they are assigned. The teams can be cross-functional and work on multiple different projects. The advantage of the matrixed structure is the efficient use of resources, better coordination, and increased information flows. The disadvantage is employees with multiple managers can be overutilized and given conflicting directions.

Employee Data

You should also obtain a staff list, which includes name, job position title, salary, and date of hire. With this information, you can determine many important factors, such as supervisor-to-staff ratios and seniority. Determine how many layers of supervisors there. Do all the staff report directly to you, or are there additional supervisors between you and the staff? This is important to determine if you will have hands-on performance reviews, direct coaching, and communication needs for managing non-management staff or not.

Prior to meeting your new Help Desk team, you should have a good understanding of staff seniority. Seniority can be based on position title or date of hire. It is important to understand feedback when you meet your team. Comments from staff that have a long history with the company can provide great context about issues but could also be complacent. The staff who recently joined the company may have experienced from another company and identify work practices that are an issue.

Supervisor to staff ratio

A significant factor in employee engagement is the supervisor-to-staff ratio. If the ratio is balanced correctly, supervisors can provide proper coaching, direction, and mentoring. Focused supervisors with correctly sized teams will allow good communication to improve efficiency and reduce issues. If the supervisor-to-staff ratio is too high, your team could suffer engagement, morale, and employee productivity issues.

So, what is the right supervisor-to-staff ratio? There are many factors to consider, such as work complexity, staff demographics, staff engagement, and budget constraints. If the supervisor is a subject matter expert for one or more technical areas, they will be engaged more in providing technical direction. This engagement is increased if the customer support provided by the staff is frequently complex and the staff has unique job function roles within the team.

The demographics of the staff will also determine the ratio. If the staff tenure average is under three years, the staff will require a higher level of coaching and work direction. If the team has a higher percentage of contractors, you may have a higher turnover and less company engagement. A higher percentage of staff working from a remote work location may require more management overhead.

Your department budget is also an important factor in determining the supervisor-to-staff ratio. The budget constraint can lead to supervisor layoffs and organizational restructure that leads to staff ratios that are higher than ideal.

For a Help Desk with complex procedures, specialized job roles, and the need for management approvals, the ratio is typically not more than 10 to 1. For a Help Desk with repetitive tasks, a generalized job role, and scripted escalations, the ratio is typically not less than 15 to 1.

Supervisor to Staff Ratio Worksheet

A significant factor in employee engagement is the supervisor-to-staff ratio. If the ratio is balanced correctly, supervisors can provide coaching, direction, and mentoring. Focused supervisors with correctly sized teams will allow good communication to improve efficiency and reduce issues. Answer the following questions to determine your recommended supervisor-to-staff ratio.

Question 1
Does the staff provide complex support assistance regularly?
__Agree
__Somewhat Agree
__Somewhat Disagree
__Disagree

Question 2
The staff's supervisor is a working manager and is a subject matter expert in technical areas?
__Agree
__Somewhat Agree
__Somewhat Disagree
__Disagree

Question 3
Staff duties require frequent management interventions, such as approvals, decisions, and escalations.
__Agree
__Somewhat Agree
__Somewhat Disagree
__Disagree

Question 4
Are there many specialists or special job functional roles on the team?
__Agree
__Somewhat Agree
__Somewhat Disagree
__Disagree

Question 5
Much of the staff work on-premise and not in a remote location such as from home?
__Agree
__Somewhat Agree
__Somewhat Disagree
__Disagree

Question 6
Many of the staff are contractors?
__Agree
__Somewhat Agree
__Somewhat Disagree
__Disagree

Supervisor to staff ratio grading

Assign the following point value to the responses and add up the total.

Agree – 1 point
Somewhat Agree – 2 points
Somewhat Disagree – 3 points
Disagree – 4 points

6 to 9 points – The staff to supervisor ratio should be less than or equal to 7 to 1.

10 to 15 points - The staff to supervisor ratio should be between 7 to 1 and 11 to 1.

16 to 19 points - The staff to supervisor ratio should be between 7 to 1 and 11 to 1.

20 to 24 points – The staff to supervisor ratio should be greater than or equal to 16 to 1.

Chapter 7:

Job Descriptions

> **Chapter Objectives**
> - Learn the importance of job descriptions.
> - Perform a review of your active job descriptions.
> - Understanding the difference of generalists vs. specialists.
> - Complete the job description worksheet.

As a Help Desk manager, one of the best ways to understand the current expectations of your staff and make improvements is to review the job descriptions used for Help Desk agents. Well-defined job descriptions are critical to defining the primary functions and duties you expect completed by your staff. Revising the job descriptions used by your Help Desk team is a valuable Help Desk process improvement activity. By updating your job description structure, you will find it easier to build a Help Desk career path and lead to performance management improvements.

A well-defined job description will describe the most important abilities and skills necessary to be successful in the role. A job description is also a good foundation to use for measuring performance. A job description will ensure the employee in the role and their manager understand the responsibilities of the position and what is expected from them. During performance reviews, the job description will provide the manager with a good foundation on what the employee's performance review should be based. If the employee is not performing to expectations, a job description is one document that provides a common set of job duty expectations the company and manager had for the employee in the position.

Reviewing job descriptions

An accurate job description will improve the result of attracting ideal candidates that meet the qualifications you are seeking. This will also lead to better hiring decisions and fewer issues down the road. A good job description will also assist HR when they are recruiting future candidates for an open position at your Help Desk.

For a Help Desk position, some of the key abilities and skills are effective communication, problem-solving, specific technical knowledge, and customer service skills.

> **Action Steps**
>
> **Job Description Review**
>
> 1. Gather all the job descriptions used for the Help Desk roles. This includes agents, trainers, supervisors and any other current role active for the Help Desk staffing budget.
> 2. Create a simple org chart on paper with each box being a role type. Represent any role type modifier such as a senior status as an additional box.
> 3. Place the number next to each role type reflecting the number of employees in that role type.
> 4. Gather compensation ranges used for each Help Desk roles.

You first should determine if there is one general job description or multiple job descriptions based on experience and special skills. Just having one general job description for the entire Help Desk staff will not promote a career path. It means as Help Desk agents season and mature in their position, they will not have the opportunity for an internal position within the team. In a mature Help Desk structure, you will see job positions have a level 1, 2, and 3 tier level experience modifier, or you may have a junior and senior level. Level 1 or junior positions will perform routine duties under direct supervision. As the staff becomes more senior, this can change to indirect supervision. Industry-standard Help Desks will have 70% to 80% level 1 or junior

Help Desk agents with a 20% to 30% of more experienced or senior level Help Desk agents.

Understanding the difference between generalists and specialists

There are two different job roles to consider when updating your Help Desk position descriptions. The first is called a generalist. Help Desk generalists possess a basic or intermediate amount of knowledge about a wide range of technical topics. A generalist is best positioned to provide first-level support to callers with issues. Most of the staff working on a Help Desk are generalists and are needed to provide the proper coverage. In the medium to larger companies, generalists are typically positioned on the front line taking the call first. If the issue is more complex, issues will be escalated to specialists or second-level support. A specialist will have an advanced or expert level of knowledge related to a limited scope of technical topics. A specialist can also be someone that has a specific role within the Help Desk or IT department. These roles could be major incident management, problem management, knowledge management, or such.

Job Description Worksheet

An effective job description will result in better hiring decisions. The right employee will make a positive impact on the team. To create an accurate and effective job description to attract the ideal candidate, follow these steps.

Step 1 - Add a job description title

Make sure your job description title is specific and clear. Refrain from using words that are too company or department-specific. For example, a good title might be the following.

Senior Help Desk Agent versus Campus Support Analyst II

Step 2 – Add a summary of the job

Qualified Help Desk personnel are in high demand. Since the job market is so competitive, you need to sell the position and your company in the summary area. Tell the candidate what makes this a great job and why they would want to work at your company. For large cities, make sure you are specific in the location of the position. Many candidates are sensitive to location for commuting purposes.

Step 3 – Add experience and qualifications

Provide a list of candidate attributes you are seeking. If it is too short of a list, you make not find the right candidate. If your list is too long, you may lose qualified candidates. Many companies will split the list into two groups such as essential and preferred. Essential might be a 2-year associate degree, and preferred could be a 4-year degree.

- Candidates will have a minimum of X years of Help Desk experience.

- Education minimum or working experience
- Industry-standard application and IT service experience – be specific and only list commonly known to the industry.
- Verbal and written communications skills
- Customer service skills
- Certifications and licenses

Step 4 – Identify the duties and responsibilities

This area is where you list the core duties of the position. This is what the performance of the employees is held responsible. Describe the daily duties of this position. Will they be mostly on the phone, or will they monitor chat sessions?

Chapter 8:

Meet with your staff

> **Chapter Objectives**
> - How to set up an initial team meeting.
> - Setting up a daily stand up meeting.
> - The benefit of weekly team meetings.
> - Starting your 1:1 meetings.
> - Career path discussions.
> - Individual and team recognition ideas

If you are a new manager, your new staff may have been self-managed, managed by a manager from a different department, or poorly managed by a former manager. Even if you have been the team's manager for a while, you must assume there are issues with staff roles, work schedules, attendance expectations, performance, and training. To build a strong team, you must be an engaged leader. It is important to set up a team meeting with your staff. Team meetings are a great way to build trust with your new staff. As you gain their trust, you will learn what may be causing some issues with your staff and the operations of the team. So, with all of these items, where do you start?

Initial Team Meeting

Being a new Help Desk manager, you may find you have a team that needs improvements. It is highly recommended to set up an introductory meeting with the entire team. An introductory meeting is an opportunity to introduce yourself and start building a supervisor-to-staff relationship. To prepare for the meeting, you should create conversation-starting questions to help the team feel confident they can share their thoughts. These questions should be focused on gaining valuable information about training, rewards, work environment, accomplishments, and improvements needed. Be sure to document the initial meeting so you can refer to the notes when later identifying gaps. Below is some good example of questions you may want to ask.

Initial Meeting Sample Questions

What obstacles are in the way of the team doing the job?
What does our team do best?
What is one thing we need to implement today to be successful?
What is one thing we need to stop doing to be successful?
What training initiative should be available for the team?
What notable things have the team accomplished this year?
What is the work environment that would allow the team to do our work best?
How do you want to be rewarded?

Daily stand-up meetings

A daily stand-up meeting is a quick 15-minute or less meeting held at the start of the shift. In a 24x7 Help Desk, you could have a daily stand-up meeting for each of the morning, afternoon, and evening shifts. Usually, a manager, supervisor, or team lead will run the meeting. Do not make this an hour-long meeting with topics that are better addressed in the weekly team meeting. As the title states, it usually is handled as a quick stand-up huddle that will quickly address the following agenda items.

Identify anything of significance that occurred during the last shift or in the last 24-hours.

Identify any significant activities that may occur in the next shift or in the next 24-hours.

Ensure the Help Desk agents have a brief opportunity to raise any concerns, impediments, or questions that need to be addressed, so they are successful in their next shift.

Weekly team meetings

Setting up and attending a weekly team meeting is very important. Once scheduled, make every effort not to cancel or miss attending a team meeting. Ensuring information is flowing up and downstream is a benefit of meeting with the team weekly. This is an opportunity to share company news and big events. Not only is it important for your employees to understand the activities in your company, but as Help Desk agents, they will most likely receive a related question from your callers.

A major portion of the meeting time may be spent discussing the team's operational performance for the week. Also, providing trending reports on the operational performance metrics is an effective way to display the performance of the team. For a Help Desk, operational performance metrics can include average call handle time, average speed to answer a call, and first contact resolution as notable examples. Discussing trends can influence better behavior and minimize negative trends in the future.

Many leaders will encourage team members to share a success story from the previous week. An example of a success story might be related to how an employee went the extra mile to help a customer with an issue. Success stories will encourage staff to increase positive customer interactions and give the team a sense of pride in their team. Sharing stories is also important when working in the technical field. A Help Desk agent must be able to draw on so much information to provide support. An opportunity for an individual to share a customer support tip learned is always positive.

The manager should wrap up the meeting by discussing upcoming events for the team and any upcoming changes to the environment. Events discussed could be a new application being deployed to the company staff as an example. An example of a change to the environment could be that the sales department is going to have a second shift added. This could drive the need to increase Help Desk support coverage during the second shift. Here is a good overall team meeting agenda;

Sample Team Meeting Agenda

Company news
Operational performance
Celebrating accomplishments
Sharing something learned
Upcoming events and changes this week

Weekly 1:1 meeting with direct reports

Weekly 1:1 meetings with your direct reports will ensure there is an alignment of expectations between a manager and employee. It also allows for ongoing performance corrections before they become big issues. Some people recommend that you allow the employee to assist with the meeting agenda. This will make sure the issues they want to discuss will be covered. Of course, there are performance items you want to cover, so keep your own private agenda list. Make sure your agenda includes some time to discuss training and career path. This will help your employees long-term. For the Help Desk, it is important you have the individual's performance against team averages in areas such as average handle time, first contact resolution, and other KPIs. It is also very important to review actual call recordings of the Help Desk agent providing support. Nothing is more powerful than an employee listening to their own support call and identifying what they did right and what improvement opportunities are present. Below is an example agenda;

Sample Direct Report Meeting Agenda

Employee agenda items
Performance review of KPIs
Call recording review
Training opportunities

Annual skip level meetings

If you do have at least one supervisor between you and your Help Desk agents, I suggest setting up skip-level meetings. A skip-level meeting is one where you individually meet with your direct report's staff to discuss training, rewards, work environment, accomplishments, and improvements needed. Skip-level meetings are an opportunity for Help Desk agents to meet with you at least once a year to give you unfiltered feedback and build a bidirectional level of trust. Before you implement skip-level meetings, you need to meet with your direct report first to obtain buy-in. Without the supervisor being onboard, skip-level meetings could look like you are diminishing their authority with their staff.

Career path discussion

Working with your direct reports to define a career path is critical for employee engagement. The career path is the growth of the employee within an organization. The career path is measured by the movement of the employee, both vertical and horizontal, within the organizational structure of a company. Horizontal movement within a company can be just as important as vertical movement. Horizontal movement can give you a broad perspective of job functions. If your career track is management, having this broad perspective can make you a more well-rounded manager.

Individual and Team Recognition

Too many managers focus just on negative employee behavior and implementing human resource approved disciplinary actions. Successful managers not only ensure they deal with negative behavior but also celebrate success or positive behavior. This celebration of success reinforces positive employee contributions and will lead to an environment that inspires an increase in employee engagement. To properly recognize performance and achievement, I have the following recommendations.

It is very important to recognize positive accomplishments when they occur. This timely recognition of positive behavior on the spot will reinforce success. Make sure the behavior or action is related to a team or organizational improvement goal. Tying this to a team or company goal is building a foundation of success in meeting the goals. Make sure the praise or award matches the behavior or action. You do not want to under or over-award but make it appropriate in scale. You should show emotion and be authentic when recognizing the behavior or action. An employee or team will know when the recognition is not authentic. The recognition does not need to be monetary. Employees want to feel valued, so a handwritten note, certificate, or team event can go a long way to achieving that. Below are a few ideas for individual and team recognition events.

Meet with your staff worksheet

Step 1 – Schedule an initial team meeting

Use the below initial meeting sample questions. Record the feedback to use for future improvement projects.

1. What obstacles are in the way of the team doing the job?
2. What does our team do best?
3. What is one thing we need to implement today to be successful?
4. What is one thing we need to stop doing to be successful?
5. What training initiative should be available for the team?
6. What notable things have the team accomplished this year?
7. What is the work environment that would allow the team to do our work best?
8. How do you want to be rewarded?

Step 2 – Schedule weekly team meetings

Create a standing weekly team meeting agenda. Below is a sample agenda.

- Company news
- Operational performance
- Celebrating accomplishments
- Sharing something learned
- Upcoming this week

Step 3 – Celebrating accomplishments

Determine how you as a manager will recognize positive behavior and outstanding performance. Below are ideas for celebrating accomplishments.

Leadership presentations

Allow an individual or team to present their achievement to leadership. If employees have been working on a successful project, formally presenting the results to leaders can be very rewarding for all.

The employee of the month

Create an employee of the month program. Make it clear what the selection criteria are to become an employee of the month.

Share feedback publicly

Send out praise received about an employee or the team. As a manager, you may receive a lot of feedback about your staff. Share the positive feedback publicly via email, team meetings, or newsletters.

Company or department newsletter

If you have a company or department newsletter, place employee achievement news in this publication. Not only will this recognize an employee, but the company or department will start to understand the great things being done at the Help Desk.

Suggestion box

A suggestion box is a great way to receive feedback, tips, or ideas. I recommend not making the submission anonymous so you can follow up with the submitter for more specific information. To encourage submissions, offer a reward if the feedback, tip, or idea is successfully implemented.

Handwritten thank-you notes

A thank you card is great. Sending a handwritten thank-you note can take it to a higher level. Personalizing the thank you note with a personal comment shows how much you value the employee and their hard work.

Peer to peer recognition

Having employees recognize each other can really provide a unique perspective on who is really performing well.

Recognition of a job well done is a fundamental need of an employee to confirm managers value their work. Once an employee feels their work is valued, engagement and productivity will increase.

Chapter 9:

Helpful Certifications for the Help Desk

> **Chapter Objectives**
>
> - ➢ Learn the benefits of having a certification.
> - ➢ Understand that a certification is only one measurement of an employee's ability level.
> - ➢ Review the list of the most common certifications related to the Help Desk.

In the world of Information Technology, there are many certifications that can be obtained. Many technology companies offer certifications for their systems and applications. These certifications focus on server administration, programming, security, ITIL, networking, customer service, and many other areas. Employee certifications recognize an employee's accumulated training and experience in a subject area.

Benefits of employee certifications

There are many benefits to obtaining a certification in information technology and, more specifically, in Help Desk-related topics. We have outlined some of the benefits below.

Career diversity

Many technology-related employees will hold multiple certifications. By holding multiple certifications, people can move within a department to perform different roles. For example, there are many roles Help Desk agents can try. These roles include incident manager, workforce manager, reporting specialist, phone administrator, and such.

Networking

By holding a certification, you can join an association based on the certification. Joining an association is good for your career path, sharing knowledge, and finding the next job.

Increased pay

Visit any certification website, and they always list one of the benefits of certification as an increased salary or pay range. Many employers will view a person with a certification as holding an above-average skill set in the area of expertise. This may allow you to obtain a salary in the middle or upper range of the salary range for the position.

Verified skill level

When you are interviewing a candidate, and you ask about the candidate's experience with a certain subject, how can you really verify their skill level? Certifications are one way to establish a minimum skill level in the subject that you're discussing. For example, if you are interviewing candidates for a project manager position and they have a project manager certification, you will know that they have a certain level of skills in that area.

Increase your marketability

Many job positions will list certifications as required or preferred. By holding a certification, you open the door to more job opportunities.

Certifications are only one measurement

Certifications may be a requirement for certain professions such as doctors, lawyers, and airline pilots. To be a Help Desk agent, holding a certification is rarely a requirement. Help Desk managers view certifications as one measurement of an employee's ability level. An employee's real-life work history is arguably more important. This includes applying the knowledge with successful and measurable outcomes is arguably the best gauge of an employee's qualifications. With that said, some of the most important certifications for the Help Desk are listed below.

Specific Certifications for Help Desk Agents

Information Technology Infrastructure Library (ITIL®) – ITIL is a framework focused on the alignment of IT services with the needs of the business. The framework allows for people and resources to have common terminology and a set of practices. The initial ITIL® certification is called ITIL® Foundations. This requires 20 hours of classroom training and passing a certification exam. The Help Desk agent will learn about topics such as incidents, problems, and change management. This knowledge will be important for understanding incident prioritization, known error handling, working with knowledge, linkages between all the disciplines, and understanding how changes impact the environment.

HDI® Support Center Analyst – This classroom training focuses on techniques for customer interactions, troubleshooting skills, call handling, active listening skills, and an overview of some ITIL® disciplines. All of the subjects taught in this course are directly related to a Help Desk agent's duties. After successfully completing the course, students can become certified by passing the exam.

Microsoft Specialist – The focus of the Microsoft Specialist and Enterprise Desktop Support Technician certifications is based on the skills and knowledge to install, configure, update, and recover Windows computers. A Help Desk agent will regularly provide support for Microsoft Windows-based operating systems. Microsoft offers many advanced certifications related to other support areas.

CompTIA A+ Certification – This certification is related to the competency of computer service professionals in configuration, maintaining, upgrading, and operating computer hardware and operating systems. While the certification is vendor-neutral, it focuses on PC hardware and peripherals, mobile device hardware, networking and troubleshooting hardware, and network connectivity issues.

CompTIA Network+ Certification

This is a vendor-neutral networking certification. Employees that have a Network+ certification have the basic knowledge of troubleshooting and managing wired and wireless networks. While most Help Desk agents do not need network skills at an administrator level, successful Help Desks will have some agents with a network background in troubleshooting basic network-related issues.

AppleCare service certifications

The two main certifications for AppleCare are an Apple Certified Mac Technician (ACMT) and an Apple Certified iOS Technician (AciT). Employees of companies who possess these certifications can allow the company to become an Apple-authorized service facility to perform warranty and repair work without voiding a warranty.

Call Center Certification

A modern Help Desk will leverage network-based phone systems with a call management controller to route calls based on programmed logic. Certifications are available for the administration, configuration, and troubleshooting of call management systems. The type and level of certification are based on the manufacturer you use in your company.

Workforce Management Certification

Workforce management is focused on the planning, staffing, and scheduling of resources to meet the customer support demand of your Help Desk. Workforce management can be a specific role or part of Help Desk management duties. There are many manufacturers of workforce management applications, and most of the major manufacturers have certification tracks that focus on labor scheduling, work data collection, leave management, and activity management.

Chapter 10:

Implementing an Employee Training and Development Program

> **Chapter Objectives**
>
> ➤ Understand the difference between training and development.
> ➤ Learn the most common Help Desk new employee training and development topics.
> ➤ Understand the best practices for creating an employee training and development program.

Managers know that company success is a result of knowledgeable and engaged workers with the skills to meet their job duties. To develop and keep top talent productive, you need a comprehensive training and development program. You often see programs call employee training and development. Both training and development are focused on improving employees' efficiency, accuracy, and performance in specific areas. However, there is a difference between employee training and employee development. While the difference may be slight, we have tried to identify what each means and identify ways to offer both.

Employee Training

Employee training is to improve workers' performance by transferring the job-specific system and process knowledge to be used in their current job position. The focus of employee training is to improve the employee's knowledge of the systems and processes used to perform the duties and requirements of their job role. For example, if an employee is in a Help Desk agent position and has a requirement to create a ticket for every support interaction, then they need to be able to do this. If they don't know how to create a ticket, then they will need training.

New Employee training topics

- Basic ticketing application use
- Fundamentals of using the phone system
- Overview of how to create a ticket
- Introduction to the knowledge base system
- Overview of the escalation group list
- VIP procedures and contacts
- Major Incident Management procedures
- Introduction to the Help Desk mission statement
- Overview of the quality assurance program
- Social media fundamentals
- Event management and monitoring procedures
- Overview of change management

Employee Development

Employee development is to advance an employee's skills and knowledge beyond what is required for their current job position. Many people describe employee development as a career path development. This also can be described as preparing the employee for their next position with more advanced skills or knowledge needed. Using our example again of a Help Desk agent's requirement to create a ticket, the employee may want to become the Help Desk ticket application administrator as a career path. To qualify to be an administrator, the employee will have to develop their skills further. These development skills are not necessary for their current role but allow them to progress into a new role.

Example employee development training topics

- Customer service skills
- Anger management skills
- Escalation management skills
- Typing skills
- Leadership skills
- Empathy trainingOverview of change management

Creating a Help Desk Employee Training and Development Program

If you manage a support team such as a Help Desk or call center, you know that your customers expect correct answers quickly. They also demand a level of customer service which meets or exceeds their expectations. Good employee training and development programs don't just happen. So how do you put together a highly effective employee training and development program?

Trainers

Trainers are the specialists that plan, schedule, and administrator of the training program for new or existing employees. Trainers will also ensure that the curriculum is refreshed and is still relevant. After performing training and on completion, trainers will update and maintain employee training records. Trainers typically will not have a fear of public speaking. They excel at providing information interactively with audiences. They are adept at recognizing when the audience is engaged and when their message is resonating with the audience.

Typically, trainers are part of or have a close relationship with the human resource department. In some cases, trainers can be directly embedded in the Information Technology department or the Help Desk team. For smaller companies, having a full-time trainer may not be possible for budgetary reasons. In these cases, a production employee may perform training duties as a secondary role.

Curriculum

The training outline and content to achieve the objectives of the training program are referred to as the curriculum. The curriculum includes teaching aids, handbooks, visual aids, webinars, and computer tutorials. When developing a training curriculum, you must ensure the curriculum is effective, is at the lowest cost possible, and results in an increase in employee effectiveness. Training can be designed to occur in different settings, such as the classroom, on-the-job, self-study, web-based, workshop, and software-based simulations. Identification of the following variables will help you to develop the overall training curriculum.

- Calculate the total number of employees requiring training.
- Identify the obstacles to scheduling training. This may include how to cover the day-to-day work.
- The number and skill level of the instructors needed.
- The methods for evaluating the effectiveness of employee training
- The training facilities and resources needed to perform the training.
- A plan on how the training record will be maintained after the training has been completed.
- The overall training costs.

New Hire Onboarding

It is important that the first impression of the new employee of your company is positive. Proper onboarding will improve their initial engagement and set a positive expectation for their new positions. A new hire onboarding training program should include;

- An onboarding agenda should include a checklist of onboarding tasks for the first week.
- Dedicated time to complete required paperwork and training
- A tour of the building and services available
- Plan a manager's meeting, such as lunch for the first day.

- Cover important work processes and safety procedures as applicable.

Ongoing training and skill development

An ongoing training program is important for employees to refresh their current required knowledge of work practices. Ongoing training will also assist employees in incrementally improving their skills. Companies will use ongoing training to keep up with industry changes and the latest technology to stay ahead of competitors. This training will also reduce skill gaps and allow employees to meet the requirements of their job description more successfully.

New process training

When things change at a company, employees need to have the training to succeed. When a company implements a new complex policy or if a new IT Service is to be introduced, specific training may be needed. The training should describe the new IT service, when it will be implemented, set expectations on how it will be used, and where to go for additional assistance.

Just in time / CBT training

The above training is great; however, employees may not internalize the information until a later time when they actually have to use it. Just in time and CBT training is a good option to provide on-the-spot training when an employee is confronted with a new application or process. This training could be provided by an in-person visit by a trainer, a computer-based training video, or a quick reference card at the employee's work location.

Employee Training and Development Worksheet

This employee training worksheet is focused on creating an effective training structure template. This training template will be generic, and you can use it to develop the training for any topic your staff needs. However, we will give you our suggestions and recommendations for training topics to get you started.

Step 1 – Identify the major training areas needed at your Help Desk.

These are top-level training programs. Our suggestions are below.

<u>Top-level training programs</u>
Ticketing application
Incident management
Monitoring and event management
Phone system
Social Media and chat support
Knowledgebase
Problem management
Change management

Step 2 – Break down the top-level training programs into smaller-sized training modules.

By creating smaller training modules, they will be right-sized and focused on the experience level of the trainee. An example of the ticketing application training program breakdown is below.
Remember, this is done for every top-level training program identified.

Top-level training program: Ticketing application
Training module 1: A training module focused on the basic ticketing application functions for a Help Desk agent.
Training module 2: A training module focused on the advanced ticketing application functions for a Help Desk agent.
Training module 3: A training module focused on creating and publishing reports from the ticketing application.
Training module 4: A training module focused on the ticketing application functions for a Help Desk team lead and manager role.
Training module 5: A training module focused on administering the ticketing application functions for a Help Desk administrator or specialist.

Step 3 – Develop learning objectives for each of the training modules.

These are the specific objective you want the trainee to understand after completing the training. Below is an example using the ticketing application. *Remember, this is done for every training module identified.*

Top-level training program: Ticketing application
Training module 1: A training module focused on the basic ticketing application functions for a Help Desk agent.
Training objective 1: Objective 1 is focused on creating and documenting an incident support ticket.
Training objective 2: Objective 2 is focused on the proper use of the ticket classification process.
Training objective 3: Objective 3 is focused on using the knowledge base, decision trees, and ticket matching to resolve tickets.
Training objective 4: Objective 4 is focused on escalating a ticket and understanding which resolver groups to use.
Training objective 5: Objective 5 is focused on how to provide ticket status updates to the customer.

Training objective 6: Objective 6 is focused on how to handle a request for service.

Step 4 – Develop the training content for each training module.

This is where you put meat on the bones. Make sure the training content is specific for each training objective. You can always add another training objective if needed. We have assembled some tips for developing the training content.

Hands-on – Make sure the training content uses hands-on exercises to reinforce the training.

Trainee participation – Make sure the training content facilitates a discussion between the trainer and trainees.

Handouts – Make sure the trainees receive handouts and other materials they can review during and after the training session.

Computer-based content – Provide videos or computer-based content and make sure the trainees can review the content as much as they want.

Step 5 – Determine who needs training.

In step 2, we had several training modules in our example. A relatively new Help Desk agent would need the training module for the basic ticketing application functions of an agent. However, they would not need the training module for the ticketing application administration. We recommend creating a training program for every employee.

Help Desk Process

Customers have an expectation when contacting the Help Desk to have a positive and consistent experience. This positive and consistent experience is not provided by the Help Desk by chance or ad hoc. The procedures used by a mature Help Desk are based on industry-standard information. This information has been developed over decades of trial and error. In this next section, we will cover a range of procedure topics. These procedure topics include setting up a phone call handling procedure. We will also walk you through creating a call and ticket quality assurance procedure. In addition, we will show you how to perform a maturity assessment, improve FCR, and discuss enterprise reporting. At the end of many of the chapters, we will provide an instructive worksheet. The worksheet is intended to assist you in the implementation of the procedure at your Help Desk.

Chapter 11:

Identity and Access Management

What is Identity and Access Management?

Identity and access management ensures the right people have the appropriate access to systems and applications to perform their work when they require it. That was a big sentence; let's break it down. When we say "right people," we mean the user's identity has been identified. The user has been authorized to receive the access. When we say "appropriate access," we mean that the user only receives enough access to perform their work. For example, general users will not receive administrator access to an application but only a limited role to perform their work.

The identity and access management process governs the management of user identities and user access to resources within an organization. A Help Desk plays a big role in the identity and access management process. The Help Desk typically executes the identity and access management actions. Help Desk agent's job duties include managing user identities, resetting passwords, and provisioning access to resources. Every company has an identity and access management process. The question to ask is how mature and secure is the identity and access management process being used at your Help Desk?

Identity and Access Management process

Do you have a formally approved and documented identity and access management process? A mature Help Desk will have a formal identity and access management process. The key word in the previous sentence is formal. Every Help Desk may be able to reset passwords. However, a mature process will have documented procedures based on security controls to ensure the process is secure. The Help Desk agents will follow the procedures step by step. This is to ensure that access is provisioned in a repeatable and secure manner.

The identity and access management process and procedures followed by the Help Desk must also be auditable. Reviews and audits of identity and access management are very common for a mature Help Desk. Since the step-by-step procedures are documented, the access provisioning can be audited easily. In addition to documented procedures, a ticket must be created. For each access request the Help Desk works on and processes, a ticket must be created. The ticket must contain important information on who, what, when, and such about the access request.

Identity and access management training

Is it mandatory that your company's employees receive training on security, identity, and access management policies? Security training for all employees is an important factor in a successful identity and access management process. A knowledgeable employee about security requirements and best practices will be able to report issues to the Help Desk as they encounter them. The Help Desk agent should receive significant training on how to recognize, document, and escalate security-related incidents. These security-related incidents can flow to a security resource for review and disposition. Security incidents can uncover vulnerabilities in a company's identity and access management process. Once security incidents are remediated, procedures can be updated. Help Desk agents and other employees must receive some form of training for the new procedure steps.

User Identification Validation

Does the Help Desk have a process to validate the caller's identity before resetting a password? Resetting a password for a system account will give the caller access to the resource. It is important to validate the caller's identity before resetting a password or performing any account maintenance. Otherwise, the Help Desk could give unauthorized access to the wrong person and cause a security incident.

In the past, establishing user identity was performed by asking the user something they know, such as prearranged challenge questions. Establishing a user's identity by solely using challenge questions is no longer recommended. Compromised user accounts are one of the primary culprits in some major data breaches. Today and beyond, user identity should be established using multi-factors. One of the factors can be something a user knows. Challenge questions would be an example of something a user knows. Additional factors used should be based on something they have (token, phone code, or security app) or something they are, such as a fingerprint or face scan. The most critical part is to ensure a process to validate the caller's identity is in place, approved, and used.

Self-Service Password Management

Do your customers have the ability to reset their passwords using a self-service tool? One of the highest call volume and cost drivers is password-related calls. By implementing a self-service password management system, a Help Desk can reduce incoming call volume. When call volume is reduced, Help Desk Managers can adjust the staffing levels and save money overall.

Every Help Desk Manager knows that users calling about account access issues are always creating a challenge for staffing levels. Users tend to forget their passwords over weekends, especially on long holiday weekends. To compound the problem, the corporate IT security team will require users to create complex passwords. Many companies do not allow repeat passwords and require special characters. Customers need the ability to manage their passwords with a self-service password reset tool. A self-service password reset tool will give customers the ability to unlock, reset, and change passwords without calling the Help Desk. Again, this will reduce call volume and overall Help Desk costs.

The Onboarding and Offboarding Workflow

Do you have an automated onboarding and offboarding process to manage permissions for new or leaving employees? Onboarding and offboarding are activities that occur repeatedly. Many Help Desks expend a lot of energy trying to set up accounts ad hoc. Having an automated onboarding process can make the process smooth and manageable. For employees that change departments or job roles at a company, many companies fail to remove the employee's legacy job role permissions. The result is the employee may have too many permissions for their new job role.

An automated onboarding process is usually driven by a workflow engine in the ticketing application or part of a security account management application. The hiring manager normally kicks off the process by completing a request form for their new hire. Selections are made in the form of the access the new user will need. Once submitted, the workflow engine will create tasks in the ticketing application for work teams.

Separate Administrative account

Do your Help Desk agents have a separate administrative account to use when elevated permissions are required? Help Desk personnel usually have elevated permission to reset passwords, install software, and navigate data repositories. Administrative accounts with elevated permissions need to be secure and controlled. A security best practice is to ensure the Help Desk personnel only have the appropriate amount of elevated permissions necessary to do their job and only use elevated permissions when necessary. To enforce security controls, many companies give Help Desk agents two accounts. The first account is their day-to-day account, where they can do most of their activities that do not require an elevated level of permission. When they do need elevated permissions, they use a secondary account that has administrator rights. Typical uses of these elevated permission accounts are used when they need to work with passwords, installs, and such.

Another option many companies are now using in security applications is an enterprise password management system. These systems allow the changing of passwords enterprise-wide when people change roles or leave the company. These security applications can manage temporary passwords for vendors and contractors. This will allow these passwords to be changed or disabled when needed automatically. Auditing account use is a very helpful option to know who used an account and when.

Role-based access control (RBAC)

Does your company have defined role-based access control permitting users access to only what they absolutely need to perform their job functions? Employees must only be allowed access to resources necessary to perform their job duties. Role-based access control is set up to define specific roles in a company, such as financial analyst or human resources generalist. Once the role is defined, permissions and security groups are assigned to that role based on the minimum access needed for someone in that role.

Access Approval Process

Does your company have a process to obtain approval from service owners and employee managers for access requests? The Help Desk can receive many access requests to resources. One identity and access management best practice are to have the resource owner approve the access request. In addition, the manager of the requestor should approve the request.

Access Auditing

Do you have a way of auditing password resets and account provisioning? Creating user accounts, resetting passwords, and delegating access to users is too easy. The administrative ability to perform these actions needs to be restricted, controlled, and monitored. Once you have your process and controls in place, these actions need to be audited. Active Directory has specific group policy settings to log password resets and account provisioning changes. The problem is the logging data is complex and difficult to be efficient in auditing. Mature Help Desks will have an internal or 3rd party application to gather, sort, and present security log data in a useful and efficient interface.

Multifactor Authentication

Does your company use multifactor authentication? User authentication to a resource by two or more pieces of evidence is known as multi-factor authentication. The evidence or factors are grouped into knowledge, possession, and inherence factor categories.
- **Knowledge** is something that only the user knows, such as a password.
- **Possession** is an object that only the user has control of, such as a token.
- **Inherence** is defined as something the user is, such as a fingerprint.

Multifactor authentication is used to make access to resources more secure. If one factor is compromised, such as a password, then access is still secure with the other factor, such as a token or fingerprint needed to access the resource.

Identity and Access Management Worksheet

Identity and Access Management

The identity and access management process governs the management of user identities and user access to resources within an organization. A Help Desk plays a big role in the identity and access management process. Help Desk agent's job duties include managing user identities, resetting passwords, and provisioning access to resources.

For this identity and access management worksheet, I am recommending implementing the following projects.

Step 1 – Define your Identity and Access Management process

Do you have a formally approved and documented identity and access management process? If you do, great. Well done.

If you do not, then you will need to start somewhere and document your current processes.

1. The best way to start is to perform a work in motion. Have an auditor monitor your team to identify all the identity and access management processes they do. This includes identifying the processes step by step. The processes should be documented by creating specific operational procedures.
2. Once documented, the procedures should be reviewed by security experts. The security experts will determine if there

are security concerns for any of the newly documented procedures.
3. The procedures must be updated with any recommendations or requirements provided by the security experts.

Step 2 – Setup Identity and access management training

Once you have your identity and access management processes defined and documented into procedures, staff will need to be trained. It should be mandatory that your Help Desk staff receive training on security, identity, and access management policies and procedures. Security training for all Help Desk agents is an important factor in implementing a successful identity and access management program. The Help Desk agent should have training on how to recognize, document, and escalate security-related incidents.

Step 3 – Ensure User Identification Validation

When a user calls the Help Desk, it is important to ensure the caller's identity before resetting a password or performing any account maintenance. In the past, establishing user identity was performed by asking the user something they know, such as prearranged challenge questions. Establishing a user's identity using challenge questions is no longer recommended. Compromised user accounts are one of the primary culprits in some major data breaches. Today and beyond, user identity should be established using multi-factors. These should be based on something they have (token, phone code, or security app) or something they are, such as a fingerprint or face scan. The most critical part is to ensure a process to validate the caller's identity is in place, approved, and used. Engage 3rd party vendors to provide a demonstration of their identification validation applications.

Step 4 - Implement a Self-Service Password Management Process

One of the highest call volume and cost drivers is password-related calls. Self-service password reset tools will give customers the ability to unlock, reset, and change passwords without calling the Help Desk. Self-service password reset tools can significantly reduce costs. To implement a self-service password management system, follow these steps.

1. **Gather the password management data.** The data needed include call and ticket data. We will need to know the volume of calls received and the number of tickets created. We will need to know the average duration of the calls and the cost per call. Other data may be needed. The goal of this step is to determine how much time and money your Help Desk is spending on password management.
2. **Research the current top password management systems available.** I recommend going to Gartner or Forrester to obtain a list of recommended password management systems. Reach out to multiple password management companies to set up demonstrations of their application. For more specific password management system information, please refer to this book's companion website, BuildaHelpDesk.com.
3. **Create a finalist list.** Setup three password management vendors to provide a demonstration and a quote for their system.
4. **Select and implement the self-service password management system.** Once implemented, you should find a reduction in call flows to the Help Desk. This should improve metrics and allow you to adjust staffing levels to save money.

Step 5 – Implement Role-Based Access Control

Does your company use defined role-based access controls to permit users access only to what they absolutely need to perform their job functions? Employees must only be allowed access to resources necessary to perform their job duties. Onboarding new users is a process that occurs repeatedly. Many Help Desks expend a lot of energy trying to set up accounts ad hoc. Having an automated onboarding process can make the process smooth and manageable. Below is a high-level list of steps needed to be completed to implement role-based access control at your company.

Step to implement Role Base Access Control (RBAC)

1. **Define the IT services you provide to your customers.** Examples of these IT services are email, applications, and file shares.
2. **Determine the roles needed for each of the IT services.** For each of the IT services, you may have different roles identified, such as an administrator, general user, and power user.
3. **Create the security groups for the IT services roles.** Access is provided by security groups. Each specific role needs to have a security group defined. Once the role is defined, permissions and security groups are assigned to that role based on the minimum access needed for someone in that role.
4. **Create business group roles.** Business group roles are set up to define specific roles in a company, such as financial analyst or human resources generalist. Then each of these roles will have whatever specific IT services roles are needed for the group to perform their job.
5. **Implement a process to onboard, offboard, and modify the user provisioning and access process.** Defining how users are placed into business roles and security groups to receive access to IT services is very important. I recommend having a workflow of resource manager approval, approvals from a user's manager, and an auditable process trail. An automated

onboarding process is usually driven by a workflow engine in the ticketing application or part of a security account management application. The hiring manager normally kicks off the process by completing a request form for their new hire. Selections are made in the form of the access the new user will need. Once submitted, the workflow engine will create tasks in the ticketing application for work teams.

Chapter 12:

Help Desk Telephone System

> **Chapter Objectives**
>
> - Benefits of a phone system.
> - Learn the components of the phone system.
>   - Agent technology.
>   - Voice over IP
>   - Computer Telephony Integration.
>   - Automatic Call Distributor.
>   - Call Recording system.
> - Phone add on tools and services available.

Customers have many different communication channels to request support from your company. These methods include chat, phone, email, social media, in person, and many other channels. A phone system is the mainstay of all Help Desk support channels. Being able to call the Help Desk is so foundational that many customers may become frustrated if calling the Help Desk is not an option.

Benefits of a phone system

Person-to-person communication – Nothing will improve customer satisfaction like a positive interaction with your customer support staff. Many customers are reporting an issue they are upset about, and empathy goes a long way to diffuse the situation.

Interaction recording – A benefit of providing support by phone is the ability to record the interaction. Call recordings are important for compliance, coaching, training, and support reviews.

Remote support – Many Help Desks currently provide remote support, which allows Help Desk agents to remotely connect to the customer's computer to resolve the issue directly. While connected remotely to the computer, it is critical to be able to speak to the customer during the interaction.

Warm transfers and conference calls – Even for a mature Help Desk, more than 30% of all calls cannot be resolved by the first agent attempting to provide support. However, there are times when the first-level agent can warm transfer the caller or conference to someone who can. Not disconnecting the call with the customer will improve the customer experience.

Providing phone support is resource-intensive

While providing this communication channel is important, it is also expensive. Providing live phone support requires the infrastructure and resources to handle the call volume. To illustrate this point, let us use an example. A Help Desk is providing IT support Monday to Friday from 9 am to 5 pm for a company of 50 people. How many agents will you need to make sure there is coverage during breaks, days off, or more than one customer call at a time? Perhaps you can get by with two Help Desk agents and two phones, but the support will be limited. Just think of the Monday morning password issues with customers all calling near the same time. The third customer calling will be on hold, receive voicemail or a busy signal. Now, what would happen if you provided 7/24/365 support? You will need to increase your staffing resources to answer calls during nights and weekends. As you can see, the workforce management of offering live-caller support via phone system can be challenging. For this reason, many Help Desks will offer additional contact channels so customers have an alternate method to request support that may be less resource-intensive.

Properties of a phone system

Properly providing live customer support via a phone system requires the use of technology systems. These systems can help managers and administrators to maximize the available workforce and minimize caller delays to receive support. Understanding what makes up the current standard Help Desk phone system is helpful to determine what is right for your company.

Agent Technology

A robust phone system can improve the productivity of Help Desk agents if correctly implemented. The technology provided to the agent will need to enable the agent to do their work. The technology needs to be reliable, easy to use, and ultimately make the agent more efficient.

Agent Headsets – If Help Desk agents are expected to be on the phone most of their day, they cannot be burdened by trying to hold a handset all day. The typical agent nowadays will have a headset. These headsets fit over or in agents' ears and have a small microphone. Some agents prefer the over-the-ear headsets to help reduce noise from their neighbors. The headset can be wired or wireless. There can be an option of answering the phone by touching the headset.

Hard phone – The headset will connect to either a hard phone or a softphone. A traditional hard phone, short for hardware-based phone, is a physical phone that most people understand. Unlike traditional hard phones connected to an analog line with the phone company, a Help Desk hard phone is connected to the data port to allow communication over the data network. A hard phone historically has better quality sound. However, a lot of improvement has been made by softphones to improve sound quality. A hard phone can have many advanced features built right into the phone and have physical buttons to use the functions. Some of these features include being able to listen to other agents' calls, transfer calls between multiple lines, and allowing to enable a speakerphone feature quickly. A hard phone may be the better option for a supervisor, trainer, or other administrative staff position. The cost of a hard phone is the highest when compared to softphone options.

Softphone – So what is a softphone? A softphone, short for software-based phones, is a phone application that runs on a computer. The main phone system application will associate the computer's IP address and MAC address with the softphone application and user profile. Typically, here is how it works. A profile for a user is created on the main phone application. The user opens the softphone client on the computer and logs into the main phone application. The computer address and user profile are associated. If any calls are directed to the user, it is sent to the address of the computer and received by the softphone client. One big advantage of a softphone is that it can be mobile. With the softphone client on a laptop, a user with an Internet and VPN connection may be able to connect to the phone system. This is great for salespeople, disaster recovery options, and virtual teams. Also, as companies design workspaces into Agile collaborating environments, a softphone is the natural choice to use. Another big advantage of a softphone is it is cost-effective. The main cost of a softphone is the license and maintenance fees. A disadvantage of a softphone is that the reliability of the softphone is associated with the reliability of the computer. Any errors, conflicts, or connection problems may cause softphone degradation or

Voice over IP (VOIP)

The human ear can interrupt analog sounds. Computers and networks understand and route digital signals. VOIP means that the sender's analog voice is converted by the phone or computer with a headset converted into digital voice packets. The digital voice packets can be routed to the receiver through the same network infrastructure your computer uses. Then the digital voice data is converted back to analog voice data so the receiver can hear it through the headset or phone. The benefit of VOIP is it can run over your data network and minimize the additional expensive infrastructure to route analog voice data. In addition, digital voice data can be easily integrated with other applications to offer your Help Desk robust caller support options.

Computer Telephony Integration (CTI)

CTI is a technology to integrate voice and data traffic which will allow an application to use that data to increase a Help Desk agent's productivity. A good example of this voice and data integration is a screen pop. A screen pop is when a Help Desk agent receives a call, and the caller's profile data is displayed on the agent's computer screen. A popular use of this function is to populate the user data directly into a new Help Desk ticket. This could save the agent time and reduce overall handle time. CTI also allows the Help Desk agent the ability to initiate, transfer, record, and conference calls from controls on their computer screen.

Automatic Call Distributor (ACD) system

An ACD will handle the routing of incoming and outgoing calls. It will ensure the calls are routed to where they need to go. This routing of calls is based on the IP addressing of the sender and receiver. In addition to point-to-point type routing, call routing rules can be set up on the ACD. Call routing rules are the process where a caller is redirected to a specific person, group, or an on-hold waiting queue based on programmed criteria. Programmed means Help Desk phone administrators can set up rules based on time, volume, location, caller selection, language, and other criteria to route the call.

Time-based call routing – Calls can be sent to different call centers based on time. If a caller in Boston calls the Help Desk at night, the ACD could have the rule to send all nighttime calls in the United States to a call center in India where it is daytime.

Skills-based call routing –Help Desks may handle support calls for multiple companies or support multiple services. Rules can be set up based on the number dialed or input provided by the caller and be sent to an agent based on their skill set and ability to handle the support call.

Least Occupied Routing – This is a popular routing rule that will route the calls to the Help Desk agent that has handled the least amount of calls at that point in time. Overall least occupied call routing is a fair way of distributing workload, but it does not give callers the benefit of routing calls based on agent skills.

Customer Profile Routing – Some Help Desks will create customer profiles and use that data to route calls to the Help Desk agent most qualified. For example, calls from callers identified as an executive in their profiles could be automatically routed to a specific person or group first.

Call Recording Systems

An important part of a Help Desk phone system is a call recording system. Each of the calls handled will be recorded for future playback and review. Call recording systems are highly configurable. Call recording can be configured by extension, department, or an entire company. Recorded calls can be attached to Help Desk ticks as an attachment. Managers can listen to the agent's live interaction with customers. They can be set up to mask the audio of protected data such as credit cards or social security numbers. There are many reasons a Help Desk may want or may be required to record their calls

Industry Regulations – Many financial service companies may need to record transactions to comply with federal and state regulations. Some regulations require calls to be recorded to validate sales confirmations, and callers have been informed of the terms of the sale. Also, call recording can provide an audit trail to ensure a company is complying with Do Not Call requirements.

Coaching – Recording the support interaction between a Help Desk agent and customers can really be helpful in performance management. Listing to support calls will provide management visibility into the tone, technical support knowledge, and customer serviceability of the agents. A key part of a customer support quality audit review program is the use of call recordings as one source of data. Management can review calls against quality audit criteria and assess the agent's performance. Calls can also be reviewed with agents as a coaching tool to improve performance.

Phone System Add on tools and services

Many advanced systems are available to make agents more efficient, and customers will have a better experience. Being able to add these services is enabled by using VOIP digital transmission, using an ACD that allows addons, and call center software that includes application APIs. Some of the additional services include items like predictive dialing, screen pop of caller's information into the ticketing system, and CRM systems that link customer background information to the interaction.

Workforce Management (WFM) – A critical process for the Help Desk is to build an agent coverage schedule that can handle Help Desk call volumes. Initially, it sounds easy, but there are a lot of variables to consider when building out a Help Desk agent schedule. Some of these variables included are call volumes, attendance patterns, agent performance, and other variables. WFM will analyze all this data to allow Help Desk management to forecast staffing needs accurately and eliminate over-staffing. An employee will enjoy the ability to offer flexible schedules based on the analysis the WFM system offers.

Interactive voice response (IVR) - This is a system where the caller can interact with the Help Desk call IVR system through the use of voice and keypad input. For example, the Help Desk call IVR system can present several options and can understand the answers from the caller either by speech recognition or the keypad number they enter. The benefit of this system is it generally reduces waiting time for the call, per call costs are reduced, and the caller can be routed to the most appropriate extension.

Chapter 13:

Implementing a quality assurance program

Chapter Objectives

- Benefits of a quality assurance audit program.
- Learn the prerequisites of a quality assurance audit program.
- Understand how and what to grade.
  - Phone greeting.
  - The support interaction.
  - The closing.
  - Support ticket review.
- How to establish an audit schedule.
- Step by step setting up a quality assurance audit program.

How do you really know your Help Desk agents are providing high-quality customer service? As a good Help Desk Manager, in addition to establishing customer contact handling procedures and providing your staff with good customer service training, you must audit agent performance. To truly find out how well your customer contacts are being handled, the Help Desk management team must implement a quality assurance audit. This audit is a program to review calls and tickets on a regular schedule using a standard methodology.

Many employees believe that auditing Help Desk calls and tickets amounts to "Big Brother" watching over the operations staff. That is far from the truth. Help Desk management typically does not want or have the time to micromanage staff. However, they do want to ensure the staff and processes are working correctly. Only by listening to the agent's interaction with the customer and reviewing the support ticket documentation can you understand how well your staff is performing.

Benefits of a Quality Assurance Program

There are many benefits to implementing a Help Desk audit program. These benefits include the following;

Increase positive behaviors – Audit data will identify positive and negative performance by Help Desk agents. The analyzed information will feed into incentive and bonus programs to reward positive behavior. The information will also be used to correct negative behavior. By performing audits on performance monthly, you will quickly see an increased occurrence of positive behaviors occur in the overall team.

Improve performance management accuracy – It is difficult for supervisors to manage staff without good agent performance information. Audit data can assist managers in having meaningful weekly and monthly performance review sessions with the team and individuals. Audits will give you hard metrics to measure and discuss performance.

Meaningful annual reviews – There will be no more relying on management instinct of who performed well over the year. The Help Desk activities can be easily tracked with metrics. Audit data will clearly identify which Help Desk Agents met or exceeded their mid-year and annual review goals.

Reduce employee confrontations – A small percentage of Help Desk agents may argue that their performance does not need improvement. Without strong performance information, some supervisors will avoid confronting poor-performing employees. With actual call recording data playback of the agent's support interaction with the customer, the agent will hear the issue being addressed. The supervisor can less time debating what happened to a discussion on actions the employee can do to improve.

Improve training programs – Audit data can be analyzed to identify negative customer support trends quickly. Once spotted, a manager can help intervene with proper coaching and training as needed. Sometimes when individual audit data is aggregated to include all agents, you may find the issues are not isolated but are occurring team-wide. By performing audits on the entire team using the same grading criteria, you can spot these team-wide trends. Team-wide trends of issue occurrence will identify procedure and training gaps in providing proper guidance. This will help adjust and mature your overall training program to correct the team-wide behavior to meet expectations.

Reduce inappropriate behavior – By auditing the calls and tickets regularly, you can proactively uncover and correct inappropriate behavior. By auditing employees, the supervisory is empowered to make corrections by coaching and training proactively. If you wait until the customer notifies you about inappropriate behavior, it could cause serious damage to your company's brand and customer satisfaction.

Getting Your Quality Assurance Audit Program Started

So how do you implement a quality assurance audit program? One prerequisite is you need to make sure that your Help Desk inbound and outbound support calls are recorded. All but the most basic Help Desks will have an Automatic Call Distributor (ACD) and call recording service available. An ACD will handle incoming and outgoing calls to make sure they follow the call routing rules that you set up. Part of an

ACD is usually a call recording and archiving system. Each of the calls handled will be recorded for future playback and review. If you do not have this service available, there are many hosted or onsite service options available. Check with your phone system engineer or vendor for call recording options available. Remember to place a front-end message on the greeting to warn your customers that all calls are recorded to avoid any legal issues.

Mandatory Support Tickets - Another prerequisite to implementing a quality assurance audit program is to ensure all customer interactions with agents are documented in a support ticket. These customer interactions to and from the Help Desk captured by a Help Desk support ticket must be mandatory and enforced by management. A Help Desk support ticket is the official record of the service provided to the customer. With any official record, important details of who the customer was, when they called, what support was provided, and any follow-up activities must be documented.

Setting Goals - Before you begin designing and implementing a quality assurance audit program, you need to set your goals for the program. By setting these high-level goals, you can drive positive behavior and better track your status. The following are examples of quality assurance audit program goals that you may want to use. Remember, you need to identify specific and measurable goals.

Customer Service Expectations - Help Desk agents must provide the customer with a high-quality customer service experience. Identify specific actions such as using the customer's name, not asking the same question repeatedly, and asking if there is anything else they can help with before ending the call.

Company Pride - The Help Desk agents must positively represent the company, the Help Desk team, and the applications and services they support. Flagging agents talking disparagingly about company policies, services, and personnel.

Communication Standards - The Help Desk agents must properly communicate with the customer as expected. Use of slang and vulgar language must be part of grading performance.

Completing the Paperwork - The Help Desk agents must create, update, and handle support tickets as expected. If a support ticket has not been created or is incomplete, it should negatively impact the overall audit score.

Getting it Right the First Call – Ensuring that the customer issue is resolved at first contact. Resolving the customer issue during the support interaction should reflect positively on the audit grade. Escalating an unresolved call and ticket when a solution is available should be a training opportunity. The audit score should reflect the improper escalation and flagged for agent training.

Security policies - Ensuring the Help Desk's security policies and procedures are followed. Any violation of security-related policies should negatively impact the agent audit score, and disciplinary action should be considered.

Getting Specific on Grading Criteria

Once you have determined your goals for the Help Desk audit program, you must identify specifically how these goals will be measured. Your goal is to develop a scorecard with specific and measurable criteria to measure performance. It is important to have specific grading criteria so expectations can be communicated, calls and tickets are evaluated fairly, and Help Desk agents can be held accountable. The scorecard grading criteria will need to have point values assigned. We recommend at least a 100-point grading system with 50% of the points for the call evaluation and 50% of the points for the ticket evaluation. There are three general areas of a customer support session. These three areas are the greeting phase, the support interaction phase, and the closing phase. Below are examples of specific and measurable criteria to grade performance in each of the three core areas.

The Greeting – Call Review Area 1 of 3

Proper customer greetings are incredibly important. A customer greeted positively will set the interaction up for success. Positive greetings, in addition to productive support calls, will lead to customers relationship improvements. When creating a quality assurance audit scorecard, the review of the greeting area is a core component. An approved greeting script should be provided to the Help Desk agent, and they should receive training on how to use the script. The script should include the following criteria.

Thanking the customer for calling – The customer has an issue, and they choose to contact your Help Desk team for assistance. Treat the customer with respect by thanking them for calling. Failure to thank the customer for calling should negatively impact the agent's audit score.

Branding – Branding is when you want to grade the Help Desk agent's use of an approved branding script. Branding could include the requirement to identify to the customer your company name, department name, and any slogan required. Failure to use the approved branding script should negatively impact the agent's audit score.

Personalize the Interaction – Not only should the Help Desk agent identify their name, but they should ask the customer their name. Once you know the customer's name, they should use it during the entire call. Failure to ask for the customer's name and not use it during the call should negatively impact the agent's audit score.

The Support Interaction – Call Review Area 2 of 3

The second call review area to audit is the support interaction or body of the call. There are some key factors to weigh when grading the Help Desk agent.

Reflect positively on the Help Desk – Help Desk agents must positively represent the organization. There is nothing more corrosive than a member of the Help Desk talking disparaging the company, the Help Desk team, and the applications and services they support. Any comments doing so should negatively impact the agent's audit score.

Acceptable language - Ensuring the Help Desk agent uses acceptable language during customer interaction is critical for a positive interaction. Vulgar, explicit, or politically biased language should reflect negatively on the agent's audit score.

Following support procedures – As your Help Desk team matures, there will be many improvements in creating knowledgebase solutions, performing root cause analysis, and creating processes on how the Help Desk agents should resolve issues. The Help Desk agent must be evaluated if they properly followed documented support procedures during the call. Taking shortcuts or applying improper solutions will lead to unnecessary escalations, extend the call handle time, and perhaps create more issues for the customer. Not using documented support procedures should negatively impact the agent's audit score.

Asking the customer to repeat themselves is negative. – Active listening is important. When the customer provides information on the issue they are experiencing, the Help Desk agent should concentrate on what they are being told. Having to ask the customer to repeat themselves or ask for information a second time should negatively impact the agent's audit score. The reason this is negative is that the customer becomes frustrated, and the call handle time is extended. Customer satisfaction and productivity are negatively impacted.

On hold / long periods of silence – Customers want to be heard and valued. Placing the customer on hold for a long period of time is definitely a negative. Also, not keeping the customer engaged with the support steps you are taking could create long periods of silence. Long periods of silence should be avoided and should negatively impact the agent's audit score.

The Closing – Call Review Area 3 of 3

While resolving the customer's issue is the primary goal of the entire interaction, the closing phase can really make a difference. Too many Help Desk agents rush through the closing phase of customer support.

Resolution Validation – Before ending the call, the Help Desk agent must positively identify that the customer's issue has been resolved or their question has not been answered.

Issue Escalation – If the issue has not been resolved, the Help Desk agent must provide the customer with some information. This information includes the ticket number, the next steps of the escalation, and a timeframe for additional support by the escalation group.

Other Customer Issues - Before ending the call, the Help Desk agent must ask the customer if there is anything needed.

Inappropriate conduct - Your Help Desk audit program grading criteria should have an exemption for inappropriate conduct of a significant nature. Any inappropriate conduct displayed by the Help Desk Agent that is counter-productive to your business and the health, safety, and welfare of your employees should be subject to disciplinary action.

Help Desk Support Ticket Review Criteria

Part of the quality assurance audit is to review the agent's support tickets. The audit performed on the recorded support call should also be performed with the corresponding support ticket. All support interactions need to have a support ticket created to capture the effort. The better practice is to select the agent's support calls for review first and then locate the corresponding support ticket. The reason for this is all calls are automatically recorded, but not every support interaction could have a manual ticket created.

Failure to create a ticket – If the Help Desk agent failed to create a support ticket related to the support call reviewed, they should immediately forfeit any points for the audit related to the ticket review. Remember, a Help Desk agent needs to create a ticket for every customer support interaction.

Miscategorized Ticket – Ticket categories provide a wealth of data mining information. The information is used for trending, proactive problem management, and so many other processes. If an agent fails to categorize the ticket correctly, it will cause inaccurate data mining reports.

Incorrect assignment group – If an issue is not solved on the first contact, then the ticket will need to be assigned to a group that has the knowledge or access to resolve the ticket. If the ticket is assigned to the incorrect assignment group, then it will have to be reassigned by the incorrect group to the correct group. This will cause excessive delays to the customer having their issue resolved.

Poor ticket documentation – Just creating a ticket shell capturing the basic information is not good enough. Poor ticket documentation will not give escalation groups or data mining teams enough information to make improvements. In the ticket description data field, the agent needs to capture the issue details and what steps they performed to resolve the customer issue.

Establish an Audit Schedule

It is important that Help Desk quality review audits are performed on a consistent schedule to ensure performance is continuously meeting acceptable standards. A consistent schedule will also allow you to identify issues quickly. An example is to perform randomly selected reviews of at least three support calls and associated tickets per agent per month. The calls and tickets will be graded using the Help Desk audit program grading criteria.

Customer Satisfaction Audit

Does your Help Desk send customer surveys out to customers after receiving support? Are there times when a member of management or a customer reports that they received Help Desk support that did not meet their expectations? One way to follow up on surveys that have a poor score or a direct report of poor performance is to initiate a Help Desk audit on the related call and ticket. By using the Help Desk audit program grading criteria, the review will be objective and unbiased. We suggest performing an audit on any customer satisfaction survey of less than 60%. This will be an effective way to coach your agent and give you the information to follow up with the customer.

Implementing a quality assurance program worksheet

This worksheet will assist you in establishing a quality assurance program to audit the performance of your Help Desk agents. The information obtained from the audit will feed into your performance management processes.

Benefits of a Quality Assurance Program

1. Increase positive behaviors
2. Improve performance management accuracy
3. Meaningful annual reviews
4. Reduce employee confrontations
5. Improve training programs
6. Reduce inappropriate behavior

Step 1 - Prerequisites of a Quality Assurance Program

Call recording - Ensure inbound and outbound support calls are recorded.

Search tools - Ensure the call recordings are searchable by date, agent, and any other important attribute.

Supporting processes - Make sure the procedures and training programs support the quality assurance grading criteria.

Support tickets - Communicate to the team that it is mandatory to create a ticket for every support interaction.

Step 2 - Create the Scorecard

When creating a quality assurance program scorecard, the first step is to create a template for the header information. The scorecard header information should document the following source items.

Scorecard Header Information
- Agent Name
- Reviewer Name
- Call recording ID
- Ticket number
- Dates – Support interaction date and audit review date

By creating a scorecard header information template, all quality audit reviews will capture the needed source information. Knowing the source of the audit data and who is performing the audit, a historical record will be created to make conversations with the agent easier.

Step 3 - Defining the Quality Audit Grading Criteria

In the body of the scorecard will be the grading criteria. Ensure the grading criteria includes the following for calls and tickets.

Call Audit Grading Criteria

The Greeting Phase
- The agent used an approved greeting script.
- The agent thanked the customer for calling
- Agent identified to the customer your company name, department name, and any slogan required.
- Agent asked for and used the customer's name

The Support Interaction Phase
- Agent overall communication reflected positively on the Help Desk team and the IT department
- The agent used acceptable language
- The agent followed all support procedures
- The agent did not ask the customer to repeat themselves
- The agent did not place the customer on hold or subject the customer to long periods of silence

The Closing Phase
- The customer validates the issue was resolved
- If the issue is not resolved, the agent provides the customer with a ticket number, next steps, and target time frame
- The agent asks the customer if they have any other issues and, if needed, creates another support ticket
- Agent displayed appropriate conduct

Step 4 – Define the Ticket Audit Grading Criteria

1. The agent created a support ticket that corresponds to the call recording reviewed. Remember, the best practice is to select the agent's support calls for review first and then locate the corresponding support ticket.
2. Agent correctly categorized the support ticket
3. Agent correctly assigns the support ticket to the correct assignment group
4. Agent properly documented the issue description and resolution steps into the support ticket.

Step 5 - Defining the Quality Audit Scoring Criteria

Once you have defined the grading criteria for the call recordings and support ticket, you must define the scoring values. Here is what we recommend.

Call and ticket quality are treated equally - The call recording and support ticket values should be equal. Fifty percent for the call recordings and fifty percent for the support ticket.

Weighting the call phases - Of the fifty percent of the total points for the call recordings, the support interaction phase should be equal to half the points. While the greeting and closing phases are important, the support phase includes significantly more criteria in scope for grading.

Ticket creation - If the agent does not create a support ticket for the corresponding call recording, they should lose all the support ticket points.

Example of a Quality Assurance Scorecard

Agent Name	
Reviewer Name	
Call Recording ID	
Ticket Number	
Support Call Date	
Date of Review	

Call Recording Review

Review Area	Possible Score	Review Score
Agent used an approved greeting script.		
Agent thanked the customer for calling		
Agent asked for and used the customer's name		
Agent overall communication reflected positively on the Help Desk team and IT		
Agent used acceptable language		
Agent followed all support procedures		
Agent did not ask the customer to repeat themselves		
Agent did not place customer to on hold or subject the customer to long periods of silence		
Customer validates the issue was resolved		
If the issue is not resolved, agent provided the customer a ticket number, next steps and target time frame		
Agent asks customer if they have any other issues and if needed created another support ticket		
Agent displayed appropriate conduct		
Call Recording Review Score		
Agent created a support ticket that corresponds to the call recording reviewed		
Agent correctly categorized the support ticket		
Agent correctly assigns the support ticket to the correct assignment group		
Agent properly documented the support ticket.		
Issue solved on first contact?		
Support Ticket Review Score		
Total Score		

Step 6 - Create a Quality Assurance Procedure

A quality assurance procedure must be created to avoid confusion. This procedure will explain what the program is, how it will be administered, and how the results will be used. The following criteria should be documented in the quality assurance procedure.

Review selection criteria
The procedure should define how Help Desk agent call recordings will be selected for review. Since the quality assurance audit will be used in the employee's performance management process, the selection process must be fair and well documented. Below are a few things to think about when defining the selection criteria.

Call recording duration. Short-duration calls are difficult to grade. You don't want to select a call for review that has a duration of less than a minute. There will not be enough content to review. Establish a selection duration threshold as part of your procedure.

Standard review – You should define in the procedure that X amount of standardly selected calls will be reviewed monthly.

For cause review – Your procedure should also describe how a "for cause" review will be initiated and how the results will be used in the overall agent performance review. Remember, a "for cause" review is when the customer returns a survey with a low score or they report they were not satisfied with the service they received.

Cross-team reviews
If you have a large Help Desk with some agents reporting to one supervisory and some reporting to another, make sure the supervisors perform audits of both teams.

Notifying and Training the Agents
Prior to starting the quality assurance program, the agents should have an opportunity to review the process and ask questions. You may want

to run a test month or quarter. This will give everyone involved an opportunity to use the process and fine-tune the process before the scores become official.

Chapter 14

First Contact Resolution (FCR)

> **Chapter Objectives**
>
> - Learn why is Help Desk First Contact Resolution (FCR) is important?
> - Understand how to measure FCR.
> - Review our recommended FCR improvement ideas.
> - Complete the FCR worksheet for measurable improvement.

First contact resolution (FCR) is the percent of customer contacts (incidents) that are solved by the Help Desk in the initial customer interaction without interruption. A successful resolution on the first contact means the issue is resolved before the customer's initial support session has ended. Historically the context of measuring FCR was for a phone call session between the customer and a Help Desk agent. In recent years, first contact resolution is now being applied to other contact channels such as emails. The current industry standard FCR for email is that a resolution is reached within one business hour of receiving a customer e-mail. First contact resolution (FCR) generally does not apply to service requests since many requests for service may require funding, approval, provisioning, or actions from groups outside the Help Desk.

Why is Help Desk First Contact Resolution (FCR) important?

First contact resolution (FCR) is one of the most important Help Desk measurements and directly ties into staffing, cost, and customer satisfaction. For example, if you have a 70 percent FCR, your organization is averaging 1.3 contacts per customer issue to resolve an issue. That extra 30 percent is usually escalated to and handled by a senior Help Desk Agent or level 2 technical resource at a significantly higher hourly rate. It also means the Help Desk Agent is unavailable to take a new contract during that time when the Help Desk Agent must contact the customer a second time. Customer satisfaction decreases as the duration of time it takes to resolve this issue increases. It is important to track and analyze contacts that were not solved on the first contact to control staffing levels, reduce cost, and improve customer satisfaction,

How to measure Help Desk First Contact Resolution (FCR)

Measuring First Contact Resolution (FCR) can differ between companies depending on whether you use Gross FCR or Net FCR. Gross FCR is where the number of contacts resolved initially is divided by all incoming contacts. This means all contacts, including hardware and other issues where there is no chance to resolve the issue on the first contact, are included. A better measurement is Net FCR, which is the number of contacts resolved initially divided by all incoming contacts for issues the Help Desk could solve on the first contact. This means issue types such as hardware replacement are excluded.

Identifying First Contact Resolution (FCR) candidates

How to identify and record customer contacts that are solved on the first contact can also differ. Two factors should be controlled when a process is in place to identify FCR. First, be consistent in the identification. Since FCR is one of the key metrics for employee performance management reporting, FCR identification has to be consistent across the entire team. Second, make sure issues being tracked for FCR are issues that are actually possible to solve on the first contact. Below are some of the methods used to identify FCR candidates.

Ticketing Application FCR logic – As ticketing applications become more advanced, automatic FCR identification methods are becoming more common. Initially, certain categories in the ticket classification scheme will be identified if they are FCR candidates. For example, software issues can generally be solved over the phone or with remote tools. Hardware issues generally will require a hands-on resolution. Once the issue is identified as an FCR candidate by the ticket category assigned, the ticketing system will measure the duration the ticket remains open and to who it is assigned. The ticketing system will automatically identify a ticket's FCR status based on the classification and if the ticket is opened and resolved by the same person within one hour. The accuracy of determining FCR can be increased by configuring the ticket classification selections to identify which ticket types should be included as FCR eligible.

Create a pivot table of ticket data – The most common way of identifying FCR statistics is to export the ticket data into a spreadsheet with a pivot table. This will allow you to group the data by an agent with a subgroup of FCR true or false. Frequently the data will be grouped by the agent to display FCR numbers or percentages by the agent. You can also use the ticket category field to filter out categories not eligible for FCR. While this initially may seem like a lot of work, you are able to learn a lot working with the exported data. Depending on which fields you have available with the exported data, you may be able to make reports by agent, date, category type, or department. This really can give you detailed trends.

Help Desk Agent FCR flagging – Help Desk agent FCR flagging is another common method of identifying and recording contacts that are solved on the first contact. Typically, an FCR checkbox or dropdown field is added to the incident ticket form. The Help Desk Agent will self-identify tickets meeting the FCR criteria by checking or selecting the appropriate answer. Since this method of identifying FCR is at the digression of the Help Desk agent, there could be some inaccuracies caused by the agent trying to inflate their FCR rate. Help Desk Agent FCR flagging is not the most accurate method to use. If you do use agent FCR flagging, then partner it with an FCR quality review program.

FCR quality review program – It is common to have a team review calls and tickets to ensure the Help Desk Agent is accurately identifying issues solved at first contact and other quality measurements. The review team will review the tickets to look for some obvious trends in misidentifying FCR. The review team will also run reports by the customer to validate that similar contacts were not made by the customer in a specific period.

Customer surveys – Some organizations may rely on customer surveys to ask the customer if the issue was resolved on the first contact. However, since a low percentage of surveys are returned based on industry averages, this may not truly represent the metric accurately.

Help Desk First Contact Resolution (FCR) improvement ideas

Once your Help Desk has implemented a process of measuring First Contact Resolution (FCR), you will build a baseline of your overall team FCR average. Also, you will start to see some other trends developing. The first trend you will see is that your Help Desk will have agents with strong FCR averages and agents with FCR averages that need improvement. Additionally, you will see high and low FCR rates for specific ticket categories. Consider the below First Contact

Resolution (FCR) improvement ideas to improve your team, agent, and specific ticket categorization of FCR rates.

Implement Total Contact Ownership (TCO) – This process is based on whoever started the initial contact with the customer owning the ticket from the cradle to the grave. The Help Desk Agent will have a vested interest to ensure the customer's issue is resolved versus just escalating it to another support team. If a ticket is escalated, the Help Desk agent will follow the progress, understand how it was resolved, and update the knowledge base for the specific issue. If the same type of issue occurs in the future, the agent will know exactly how to resolve the issue, and you will see FCR rates improve.

Implement skill-based contact routing – For a Help Desk with a smaller staff size, agents must have general support knowledge for almost every type of issue. For medium and large staffed Help Desks, agents develop intermediate and expert level knowledge for specific topics. By implementing contact criteria such as an interactive voice response (IVR) phone menu selections, contacts can be routed to Help Desk agents with the most applicable skill sets to resolve their issues. We call this skill-based routing. If this is correctly implemented, it will lead to a significant improvement in FCR.

Incident categorization scheme – An incident categorization scheme is a method used by the Help Desk agent to classify the support ticket based on the specific issue being reported. The Help Desk agent will listen to the customer describing their issue and then assign an incident category that best matches the issue. Once a support ticket has an incident category assigned, many ticketing applications can present highly relevant knowledge solutions based on the category selected. Presenting relevant solutions to the Help Desk Agent during the diagnosis and troubleshooting phase will lead to higher resolution and FCR rates. If no relevant solutions exist in the knowledge base for the issue, one can be created once the solution is determined. This will assist agents in the future and ultimately improve FCR rates going forward.

Caller ticket history – Issues can develop as a result of change activity. Displaying the contact's previous tickets can provide some clues to what has happened to a customer's technology recently. By presenting a summary of previous support tickets, Help Desk agents can better understand the issue the customer has been having and, if related, could help solve the current issue.

Incident decision trees – A decision tree allows employees to follow step-by step-procedures to bring incidents to resolution quickly. By inputting attributes of the customer issue into a decision tree, the Help Desk agent walks through a decision tree to the most probable solution.

Research on FCR trends – Using the Pareto Principle against the tickets not resolved on the first contact, 20 percent of those issues will account for 80 percent of the tickets. In other words, most of the tickets will be related to a small number of category types. Export your support ticket data for all issues that could not be solved on the first contact. Group all of these tickets by support ticket classification type. Arrange the sorting of the groups by highest to the lowest occurrence. Focus on the highest occurring support tickets that could not be resolved on the first contact. Identifying a solution for these issues first will significantly reduce the volume in the future.

Help Desk agent access and tools – Ensure your Help Desk Agents have the right tools and access to do their job. This sounds simple, but you would be surprised to find out that the Help Desk sometimes is not given the tools and access needed to fix the issue. The administrators of the system may not have delegated the rights to use the tool or provided the training. If this is the case, empowering the Help Desk agent with this ability will not only improve FCR rates but will free up more expensive resources to do other work.

Employee Driven Solutions – Encourage your Help Desk agents to suggest solutions to improve FCR percentage. By asking Help Desk agents for their input, they will have a sense of ownership in the process. Since the agents are part of the support calls, they may have some good improvement ideas to share. Setting up a recognition program for good ideas will also encourage participation.

First Contact Resolution (FCR) Improvement Worksheet

Goal

Improve the First Contact Resolution (FCR) rate of 10 high-volume customer issues that are currently experiencing low FCR rates.

Benefits
- Improved FCR rates
- Reduce cost per ticket

Prerequisites

Before implementing first contact resolution improvements, the following information should be gathered or understood.

Every resolved ticket has an FCR status – Our analysis will be focused on tickets not resolved on the first contact. If the FCR status by ticket is not exportable to our working spreadsheet, then we can manually perform this in the spreadsheet. We will discuss the manual process later in the worksheet.

Determine the average hourly rate for Help Desk agents – The Help Desk average hourly rate will be used when comparing the staffing costs between tickets resolved and not resolved on the first contact. To find the average Help Desk agent hourly rate, take the sum of all rates, and divide it by the number of staff.

Determined the average hourly rate for escalation groups - The escalation group average hourly rate will be used when comparing the staffing costs between tickets resolved and not resolved on the first contact. To find the average escalation group hourly rate, take the sum of all rates, and divide it by the number of staff. The basic escalation group rate is just one average hourly rate for all groups. These escalation groups may include developers, engineers, and administrators. Putting everyone into one group to find an average hourly rate is probably the best way to start. In the future, you can get more granular by calculating a per escalation group average hourly rate.

Time spent working on resolving a ticket – For our analysis, we need to know how long the Help Desk and escalation groups spent on the resolution of the incident. This data varies greatly between companies and their ticket handling processes. The ideal situation is for the Help Desk agent and escalation group members will enter a value of how much time they spent working on each ticket. If this information is not available or accurate, then you can create a time spent formula to use on all the ticket data. The formula most helpful is the following.

- **Time Spent on tickets not resolved on the first contact**
- **Help Desk time spent** - Difference between the time the ticket was created and the time the ticket was escalated.
- **Escalation group time spent** - Difference between the time an escalation resource was assigned to the ticket and the time the ticket was resolved.

Step 1 - Perform a query for all tickets resolved in the last six months.

Be sure the query parameters include capturing the below ticket data field attributes. If not all attributes are available, we will show you how to collect alternative data in later steps. This may help you find a workaround or another data field to export in its place.

Ticket Data Fields
- Ticket number
- Ticket created by name or ID
- Ticket resolved by name or ID
- Ticket classification type
- First Contact Resolution (FCR) status
- The escalation group name.
- The work start time for the escalation group and when they started to work on the issue.
- Time spent working on the ticket by user or group
- Ticket created time and date
- Ticket escalation time and date
- Ticket resolution time and date

Step 2 – Export the data into a spreadsheet.

Export the data out of your ticketing application or repository. Working in a spreadsheet will allow you to perform pivot tables, sorting, grouping, and filtering as needed.

Step 3 – Validate you have a populated column displaying the resolved on first contact status as true or false.

If you do not have the FCR status automatically identified by the ticketing application, you can use the following method.

FCR determination option – For each ticket row, note FCR as true if it meets the following criteria. The username or ID is the same for the *ticket created by* and *ticket resolved by* fields, AND the duration between *ticket created time* and *ticket resolved time* fields are 1 hour or less. If the ticket does not meet the criteria, then note FCR as false.

Step 4 – Filter your spreadsheet to display only tickets where the FCR status is false.

In this step, we want to focus on tickets where the FCR status is false. The FCR false tickets are the targets for FCR improvement.

Step 5 - Create the following new columns in your spreadsheet

- **Help Desk labor cost**
- **Escalation group labor cost**
- **Total labor cost for tickets with FCR as false**
- **FCR labor cost savings**

Step 6 – Calculate the Help Desk labor cost per ticket.

Calculate the *Help Desk work time* in minutes by finding the difference between the *ticket created time* and *ticket escalated time* fields. Calculate what the average Help Desk rate is per minute. Then multiply the Help Desk work time in minutes by the Help Desk average rate per minute.

For example, the Help Desk's average rate per minute is $0.333 (equals $20 per hour), and the Help Desk's work time was 30 minutes. The total cost of the Help Desk resource working the ticket would be $9.99.

Step 7 – Calculate the escalation group labor cost per ticket.

To calculate the cost, start by figuring out how many minutes the escalation group worked on the ticket. The *work in progress* time is the difference between the *escalation group start work time* and the *ticket resolved time*. Then multiply that time in minutes by the rate of pay per minute of the escalation group.

In our example, the escalation group's average rate of pay is $0.833 per minute ($50 per hour), and the difference between the *escalation group's start work time* and *ticket resolved time* was 30 minutes. The escalation group cost would be $24.99.

Step 8 – Calculate the total labor cost for tickets with FCR as false.

To calculate the total cost for tickets with FCR as false, add the Help Desk cost ($9.99) and the escalation group cost ($24.99). Using our example, the total cost for tickets with FCR as false is $34.98.

Step 9 – Calculate the FCR labor cost savings.

This would be the cost savings if the ticket did not have to be escalated.

Option 1 - The conservative time estimate scenario for FCR cost would be the Help Desk time worked plus the escalation group time worked multiplied by the Help Desk average rate. For our example this would be ((30 min + 30 min) X $0.333 per minute) = $19.98. **The FCR labor cost savings would be $15 ($34.98 - $19.98).**

Option 2 - You could also use the Help Desk labor cost as the cost of an FCR true ticket. For our example this would be ((30 min X $0.333

per minute) = $9.99. **The FCR labor cost savings would be $24.99 ($34.98 - $9.99).**

Either way, using option one or option two, there is a significant amount of savings to be had by improving the FCR rate.

Step 10 - Perform the calculations on the spreadsheet.

If you have not done so already, complete the previous steps on the remaining tickets. Update the appropriate columns with the information. These steps include the following.

1. Calculate the Help Desk labor cost per ticket
2. Calculate the escalation group labor cost per ticket
3. Calculate the total labor cost for tickets with FCR as false
4. Calculate the FCR labor cost savings

Targeting your FCR improvement project

Many managers will look at the FCR cost savings total and realize that there are huge cost savings to be had. In this section of the first contact resolution improvement worksheet, we will present you with a way to prioritize those improvement efforts. To determine which categories to focus our improvement effort towards, we will group the tickets with FCR as false by classification type. Then we will find the average cost savings. We will use this information to make some decisions.

Step 1 – Group data by ticket classification type.

Grouping your tickets with FCR as false by ticket classification type will provide some very useful information. I suggest using a pivot table and grouping your ticket data by your tier 2 or tier 3 ticket categories.

Step 2 - Average the costs by ticket category.

Some ticket category groupings may have hundreds of tickets. The cost per ticket may vary with the duration the ticket has been open and worked. Finding the average cost per group will give you more accurate cost information. For each ticket category group, have your pivot table show you the average Help Desk labor cost, escalation group labor cost, cost of the tickets with FCR as false, and FCR labor cost savings.

Step 3 – Determine the volume of tickets by category

This step is important. If you have a ticket category with significant average FCR cost savings, but there are only 1 of those tickets in 6 months, it may not be the highest priority to fix. Identify the ticket categories with the highest volume of tickets.

Step 4 – Select the top 10 categories for FCR improvement

In this step, you will determine the ten categories you will focus on first for the FCR improvement project. The selection of the top 10 should be based on significant volume and FCR total cost savings.

Step 5 – Create an improvement action plan

Now that you have identified the top 10 categories for FCR improvement, it is time to create an action plan project for each. Overall, the action plan will include meeting with the Help Desk and the escalation groups. These groups should figure out how the Help Desk can be empowered to perform the resolution actions the escalation group performed.

Step 6 – Measure your improvements

You have a baseline of your overall FCR and FCR by category. Continue to collect and measure monthly data to determine if you are improving. For the top 10 categories, you will start to see the Help Desk FCR rate increase. This means the lower-cost resources are resolving the issues without escalating to higher-cost groups.

Chapter 15

Performance Reporting

> **Chapter Objectives**
>
> ➤ Learn why is Help Desk performance reporting is important.
> ➤ Understand the cost per contact.
> ➤ Review what customer satisfaction is.
> ➤ Learn metrics to measure agent performance.
> ➤ Review customer call metrics.

Key performance indicators (KPI) are used by management to understand how the team is performing. It is important to ensure you are capturing accurate data to measure, manage, and implement continuous improvement efforts. Most of your data will come from your phone system, ticketing system, customer surveys, and Help Desk audit program scorecards. Performance reporting is not just one snapshot of a point in time but a trend of all those points in time to determine trends. By comparing the trend data, you can identify the strengths and weaknesses of your Help Desk. It also will allow you to compare your performance reporting against industry standards.

Cost per Contact

As a manager of a Help Desk, it is very important to understand the cost per contact. Cost per contact is the budgetary cost of operating the Help Desk and dividing by the total number of contacts. Remember, customer contact is a term used to describe a customer contacting the Help Desk by any means. Many mature Help Desks will slice and dice these numbers into different categories. You can further break contacts into subgroups such as contact by specific channel phone, email, chat, and such. You can also divide contacts by who handled the contact or resolved the issue. Some of the more popular costs per contact are:

The overall cost per contact – This metric is the baseline cost per contact report. This report is all the Help Desk expenses such as salaries, equipment, and capital divided by total contacts. This metric is useful. It gives you a per unit contact cost as a baseline.

Help Desk staffing labor cost per contact – This metric is all the Help Desk salaries divided by total contacts. A frequently used subgroup of this report is the staffing cost divided by the total number of contacts that had their issue solved at first contact FCR.

Escalated labor cost per contact – This metric is the cost of the time escalation groups expended working on issues escalated from the Help Desk. The accuracy of reporting this metric depends on some variables. To increase accuracy, you need to have a function in the ticketing application that measures how much time resolvers spent working on each ticket. You also need to know how much per hour escalation groups cost. This metric is important to determine the extra cost incurred by having to escalate issues to 2nd and 3rd-level resolver groups versus a lower-cost per-hour worker at the Help Desk.

Customer Satisfaction

An important metric for the Help Desk is customer satisfaction (CSat). Customer satisfaction is a measurement created from direct feedback from the customer on their most recent interaction. Direct feedback is obtained by offering the customer a survey after a support ticket has been resolved. The brief survey questions should focus on the knowledge, professionalism, and soft skills of the Help Desk agent. You can also ask questions related to the service received, timeliness, and satisfaction with the result. Using a survey tool that is integrated into your ticketing system will allow you to run customer satisfaction reports based on agents, issue type, and trending tickets. The customer satisfaction score by an agent is a popular metric to use in performance reporting and annual employee reviews.

While customer satisfaction survey results are an important metric, the data does have limitations. Industry-wide survey return results average only 30%. This means you are only getting satisfaction feedback from about a third of the customers. To take this a step further, you must consider what type of customer is responding. Some customers may only respond to a survey only if they are upset or dissatisfied with the service. It is recommended to use surveys as one of many data points to determine overall customer satisfaction.

Agent performance

Agent utilization - A way to keep costs per contact down and measure productivity is with the agent utilization metric. Agent utilization measures the percentage of time the agent is working. Basically, you take the total handle time of all calls handled by the agent divided by the total time the agent is working. For example, if an agent works an eight-hour shift, and their total call handle time is 5 hours, then their utilization is 62.5%. This means 37.5% of the time, the agent was waiting for a call, on break, in a meeting, and such.

Agent occupancy - Occupancy is very different then agent utilization. Agent occupancy is the time the agent is on a call or in wrap-up divided by the total time the agent is logged into the phone system. Occupancy is a metric that shows the percentage of time the agent is handling customer calls versus waiting for their next call. When comparing occupancy to industry standards, you must factor in the Help Desk staff size and call volume. A smaller Help Desk with a lower volume of calls will have a lower occupancy rate versus a large Help Desk with a large volume of calls. For example, a four-person Help Desk may have a flood of calls at 8 am but very few calls later in the morning. With a staff of four, it is difficult for a manager to be flexible staff schedules. With a large Help Desk with many agents, you can slot the schedule of agents based on call volume to maximize occupancy.

Average handle time (AHT) - This metric is the average duration of Help Desk agent hold time, talk time, and related tasks that follow the call. Average handle time is directly related to Help Desk agent performance. Too low of an average handle time may point to over escalation due to a lack of troubleshooting. Too high of an average handle time can point to a need for agent performance issues and require training and coaching.

Customer Call Metrics

Average Wait Time – Average wait time of callers waiting in the queue for the next available agent. The average wait time metric is critical for management to determine the optimal staffing levels. While average wait time is not a direct metric for agent performance, a customer wait time that is high will impact the customer satisfaction metric. Customer satisfaction is an agent performance metric. Long wait time is negative for customers, and it directly relates to customer satisfaction. If a customer's call is answered within 30 seconds, the customer should be satisfied and not upset. However, if the customer must wait 5 minutes for the next available agent, then they can be frustrated. When the next available agent takes the call, the interaction is off to a bad start with an upset customer. If the average wait time is too high, customers will see the abandonment rate significantly increase as a result of the customer disconnecting from the call.

Call Abandon Rate - The call abandonment rate is where the caller hangs up before they are connected to a help desk agent. This means the caller may have been experiencing a long hold time. To calculate the call abandonment rate, you take the number of abandoned calls and divide it by all calls offered to the Help Desk. If the abandoned rate is too high, the caller may be pretty upset with the long hold time. Keeping the average wait time in the queue down to a minimum will also help improve your call abandoned rate percentage.

Help Desk Performance Reporting Scorecard Worksheet

The goal of this worksheet is to analyze the current and previous budgets for the Help Desk. Then you must determine where additional funding should be allocated in next year's budget. The worksheet is a high-level guideline to get you started thinking about improvements as you continue through this book.

Step 1 - Analyze the budget

Implementing improvements can cost money in the short term. However, in the long-term, improvements will save you money. The goal of analyzing the budget is to find some savings without just slashing the staffing amount. You may not be able to use the budget savings directly, but it is easier to get new expenditures approved when you identify the source.

Step 2 - Identify budget savings to fund improvements

Break out the Help Desk's budget in high-level buckets if it is not already. Typical budget buckets are staffing costs, professional services, license maintenance costs, and such.

Staffing costs – Savings can be found by becoming more efficient using the process improvement ideas throughout the book. As your agents and processes become more efficient, you may be able to trim your staffing budget through attrition. For now, let us assume your staffing budget will remain flat.

Professional service – Now is the time to review your current professional service expenditures. You may have contracts in place with vendors for printer maintenance and other services, but it is never too soon to reach out to their competitors. See what another company can offer and the cost of that service. While you may not be able to change vendors immediately, you can leverage the knowledge to renegotiate your current contract.

License and maintenance costs – The hidden cost for all applications is long-term support costs. License and maintenance costs can add up quickly. Ensure your support coverage reflects what is needed versus excessive unneeded coverage. Work with your vendors to ensure your costs in this area is at the correct level required by your business needs.

Step 3 - Review performance metrics

Gather metrics used to analyze the performance of the Help Desk. These metrics may include the following listed below. Don't worry if you are not tracking all these metrics. We will discuss these throughout the book to give you information on what they are, how to track them, and how to implement improvements.

Customer satisfaction surveys (CSat) – Csat is a metric to measure the customer's approval of the support they received. Commonly a survey can be used to obtain feedback from customers after completing a support interaction.

Average Handle Time (AHT) - An average of the handling time of all calls. Handle time of a call is the sum of talk time and after-call work.

First Contact Resolution (FCR) – First contact resolution is the ability to solve the customer's issue during the first interaction without calling the customer back or transferring the customer to another agent.

Average Speed of Answer (ASA) – Average speed of answering the call is the total length of customer wait time in queue divided by the total number of calls. The phone system will calculate these metrics by agent and team.

Cost per Ticket - Help Desk agent salary cost divided by the number of tickets created.

All other useful metrics – In our discussion, we used CSat, AHT, FCR, ASA, and Cost per Ticket. When you build your scorecard, you can include these or modify the metrics used based on your needs.

Step 4 - Create a performance scorecard

Create a basic performance scorecard using a spreadsheet or other application. On one axis, enter the performance metrics. On the other axis, enter metric reporting time periods such as monthly, quarterly, and annually. See figure 2.1.

	Example Basic Performance Scorecard								
	Target	Jan	Feb	Mar	Q1	Apr	May	Jun	Q2	Additional Time Periods
Csat									
AHT									
FCR									
AWT									
Ticket Cost									
Additional Metrics									

Figure 2.1

Set a target goal - Determine a target goal for each metric. The target goal should not be a stretch goal but the minimum target needed for acceptable performance.

Analyze current performance – Review the most recent performance metrics against the target goal you set.

Performance trends - Analyze the performance metrics trend by month and quarter. Some people add arrows to the trend as compared to last quarter.

Example Basic Performance Scorecard									
	Target	Jan	Feb	Mar	Q1	Apr	May	Jun	Q2	Additional Time Periods
Csat	3.5	3.5	3.6 ↑						
AHT	4:30	4:22	4:10 ↑						
FCR	75%	76%	77% ↑						
ASA	0:20	0:20	0:22 ↓						
Ticket Cost	$3.00	$3.50	$3.15 ↑						
Additional Metrics									

Improvement planning - Determine the areas that need improvement. In our example, we see ASA has a negative trend. Also, ASA and ticket cost is not meeting the target goal. These areas should be investigated to determine what resources and improvements are needed. Use the information provided in upcoming chapters to create an improvement plan.

Investment funding - Based on the improvement plan created, determine additional funding requests needed for next year's budget.

Chapter 16

Social Media Strategies

Chapter Objectives

- Learn why understanding social media at the Help Desk is important.
- Understand the benefits of social media support.
- Learn the components of social media support.
- Discuss some of the popular social media channels.

If your Help Desk only provides internal customer support, you may not need to use social media. While the principles in this section may be relevant, using Facebook and Twitter may not be allowed for internal customer support. This chapter is mainly focused on external customer support with social media.

A forward-looking Help Desk must now have a social media strategy for external customers. Providing external customer support service via social media is growing. Customers are using social media to ask technical questions, complain about products or services, and report service interruptions. Many customers expect and demand that a company respond to their social media requests, comments, and feedback with a timely response. Not only do customers expect the response on the same platform channel, but they want real-time solutions.

Consolidated Help Desk Multi-channel support

Today most Help Desk ticketing applications support multi-channel integration to bring all your customer contact channels into one platform for seamless handling. Remember, a contact channel is a communication pathway available for a customer to report an issue to the Help Desk. These contact channels include phone, email, chat, and social media. If a customer uses Twitter to tweet a question or comment about your company, products, or services, the interaction stream can be captured inside a Help Desk ticket. When a Help Desk Agent provides a response or solution to the customer's tweet, it is provided through the same medium.

Benefits to Help Desk Social Media Support

Cost-effective – The infrastructure cost of social media support is low or free. Most social media channels are free, and only an Internet connection is needed. Some costs could be incurred with an enterprise account or a 3rd party application to aggregate the social media data into a manageable view with automated tools. Social media support is very inexpensive as compared to the infrastructure cost of phone support. As an example, with phone support infrastructure costs, you may need to invest in switches, routers, headsets, phones, licenses, an ACD, and toll-free numbers.

Customer satisfaction – A growing segment of customers expect customer support in a digital format and immediate. Designed correctly, customer support via social media can meet those expectations. Meeting customer issue support expectations can boost the customer's overall satisfaction.

Better workload management – Providing customer support by a phone call is a sequential support method. This means an agent can only assist one customer at a time. With social media, you can have several active communication sessions open at a time. Furthermore, there are many secondary views of the interaction with the primary requestor. For example, if a customer tweets a question to the Help Desk, and they respond with a solution, many other customers may see the solution also. Many time-consuming customer support phone calls may be avoided in our example. Offering social media support options means that Help Desk management can smooth their peak call volume periods.

Increased sales – For external customer sales support, if customers don't get their questions answered immediately, they could quickly move on to other vendors. Social media interactions move quickly and must occur in near real-time to be effective. Don't let your customers leave you for competitors by not responding.

Components of Social Media Support

Setting up your Help Desk team to be able to handle social media support requires some planning to be effective. There are some similarities with setting up phone support teams, but there are also some differences. Let's take a look at some of the basics.

Help Desk Ticket – The Help Desk industry standard is that every interaction with a customer must be recorded into a ticket as the official record. However, manually creating a support ticket for every social media interaction would be resource-consuming. Automatic support ticket creation is solved with technology. Most Help Desk ticketing applications now include APIs for social media services. An API is an interface pathway to allow two platforms to communicate with each other. More advanced options may require some configuration or programming.

Rules-based ticket routing and assignment – There are many social media channel platforms. Within each platform, there are many channels or lines of communication. You can group your agents by subject matter platform expertise or specific channel focus. Ticketing platforms can be configured to route new issues or questions from social media to specific agent groups. This is skilled based routing with social media.

Pulse on customer feedback – Relying solely on customer feedback surveys may leave your company without important customer support information. Social Media provides a raw and immediate pulse on how your company is doing.

Twitter

Using Twitter at your Help Desk for external customer support has some huge advantages. It is a cost-effective contact channel. The startup cost for using Twitter is minimal, and you can defer the costs of more advanced Twitter application suites until you build a large following. The flow of short nuggets of information to and from customers is rapid. You can interact with your customer base in real-time. Using Twitter can help promote your brand.

To get started on Twitter, you need to create a Twitter handle and profile. The handle is the unique name of your only presence that customers can use to include your company in a tweet. It is also the account displayed when you send a tweet. A tweet is a short message sent on Twitter. You can create specific keyword search streams to track Twitter mentions and direct messages, enabling your Help Desk ticketing platform to create a support ticket. This Twitter integration lets you engage in selected conversations across your current and potential customer base. Multi-channel support offers customers many avenues to make requests. The support your Help Desk Agents provide must be consistent, accurate, and repeatable across all channels. Implement a single repository of knowledge across your Help Desk Multi-channels and organization. Require all Help Desk Agents to provide customer support using and maturing the solutions directly from the knowledge base. With Twitter, you are allowed a limited number of characters. Your tweet response will be a specific and to the point message and should also include a link to your public-facing self-service portal.

Facebook

Over a billion people use Facebook to connect and share the things. Your company may already have a Facebook for a business page. Many of the external customer interactions may be related to support questions. With Facebook, you can integrate your ticketing system to convert your Facebook messages and wall posts to support tickets. This will allow customers to submit issues via Facebook, using direct messages and posts. A gatekeeper can route Help Desk support questions from customers to your Help Desk. Responses for Facebook posts can be automatically added both as a conversation to the customer's post and threaded to the ticket.

YouTube

This service is a video-sharing website that allows users to upload, view, share, rate, and comment on videos. There is no cost for using YouTube since its revenues are generated from advertisements. The YouTube homepage for your video is called a channel. You can customize the look and feel of your channel to fit your own branding ideas. Video-sharing can be an important platform for a Help Desk providing external support. You could post how-to support videos for your products or services. Any content you post can be commented on, which will allow you to see direct feedback and respond. Some customers prefer watching a video to obtain support information. With the videos, they can see the product or service and the steps to solve the issue visually.

LinkedIn

LinkedIn is a social networking service that is oriented toward business and professional networking. While this is a good resource for employers and job seekers, how does the Help Desk play a role?

Companies can post articles, press releases, and product information on LinkedIn. All these posts or shares can solicit positive and negative comments. Your Help Desk software can be integrated with LinkedIn to create a ticket each time a comment is made. Your Help Desk can perform the role of a monitor to ensure these tickets are routed to the correct department in your company to respond to these comments as needed.

Conclusion

Advances in Help Desk social media support platforms have to enable customer support centers to respond to customers immediately. These responses are not only requests for service but comments and feedback on social media forums. Unifying support from one platform allows Help Desk Agents to cover multiple social media channels in one view. This ability to view and respond to social media in one view decreases the per-contact cost. Companies embracing a social media support strategy have benefited from their brand, sales, and support improvements.

Chapter 17

Help Desk Ticket Classification

> **Chapter Objectives**
>
> - Understand what ticket classification is.
> - Learn why we use ticket classification.
> - Understand the benefits of ticket classification.
>   - Cost savings.
>   - Improved incident resolution.
>   - Major incident management handling.
>   - Issue avoidance.
>   - Enterprise reporting.
>   - Agent training.
> - Complete the ticket classification worksheet to build your new ticket classification scheme.

You hear a lot about Help Desk ticket classification, but what is it? Help Desk ticket classification is a method of organizing support tickets based on the attributes of the customer's issue or request. A support ticket is what a Help Desk agent creates to document the support interaction with a customer seeing assistance. The customer will explain the issue they are having, and the agent will select the appropriate ticket classification terms based on their description. Ticket classification is used as source data and input by many support processes. These support processes assist the agent in finding a resolution, reporting, and eliminating reoccurring infrastructure problems. If ticket classification is correctly set up, the Help Desk can mature many of its processes and services. Ultimately this will save money, time, and effort for everyone.

The most common ticket classification scheme is based on three levels of keywords. We call this a three-tier ticket classification structure with a parent-child relationship. Understanding the parent-child relationship is important. Each tier 1 term have its own set of tier 2 keyword associated with the tier 1 term.

Tier 1
Tier 2
Tier 3

When assigning a ticket classification to a support ticket, the agent selects from a drop-down list the most appropriate tier 1 term for the issue described by the customer. Once the tier 1 term has been selected, the tier 2 selections will become available to select. Only the tier 2 terms that are a direct child of the specific tier 1 term selected will be visible. Tier 3 is the same as tier 2. Once the tier 2 term has been selected, the tier 3 selections will become available to select. Only the tier 3 terms that are a direct child of the specific tier 2 term selected will be visible.

One important point to remember is that even though each parent tier has its own terms in their child tier, they may not be unique. For example, a tier 1 term of **printing** may have a tier 2 term of **install**. A tier 1 term of **email** might also have a tier 2 term of **install**. Both tier 1 terms are associated with the same tier 2 term.

Why do we use Help Desk Ticket Classification?

Help Desk ticket classification is used to organize support tickets. Other than to keep tickets in a neatly organized system, why should we do it? Ticket classification is such a big factor in the Help Desk's success. When support tickets are organized properly, it saves money and improves issue resolution metrics. Help Desk ticket classification is an input for other support processes. Let's try and answer why to use the Help Desk ticket classification by starting with saving money.

Cost savings - Time is money. Having an unorganized support ticket repository wastes a lot of time. The cost per ticket rises significantly the more time your Help Desk is juggling too many open and unresolved support tickets. The increased ticket handling efficiency of using a ticket classification scheme is important not only for cost-effectiveness but also for achieving positive customer satisfaction results. In many of the major Help Desk reporting metrics, controlling time is always a factor for success. For example, Average Handle Time (AHT) is the average duration of Help Desk agent on-hold time, talk time, and call wrap-up tasks that follow the call. Average handle time is directly related to Help Desk agent performance. Ticket classification can reduce AHT and save money.

Improved incident resolution - Every Help Desk needs a ticket classification scheme to properly handle the customer's issues when they contact the Help Desk for support. Searching haphazardly for a solution to resolve a customer's issue while they wait is just bad service. Applying proper ticket classification immediately when a Help Desk ticket is created enables the Help Desk Agent to leverage more advanced resolution enabling tools. These resolution tools, such as decision scripts, just-in-time knowledge, and ticket matching, will improve the Help Desk Agent's ability to find a resolution or properly route escalated tickets. By quickly resolving the customer's issue, the agent can pick up the next waiting call. Everyone is happy and satisfied!

Major Incident Management – Ticket classification is a major component of building a mature and responsive major incident management process. A major incident is an incident that demands a response and resource engagement level well beyond the routine incident management process. A major incident is assigned a critical priority based on an incident priority matrix of impact and urgency. A ticket classification scheme will allow the incident management team to assess the impact and urgency of an incident.

Issue avoidance - Resolving an issue is great, but what if you could help customers avoid the issue altogether? Proper ticket classification is a necessary input for the problem management process. Problem management is the life cycle process of identifying, investigating, documenting, and permanently resolving incidents caused by problems in the production environment. Applying proper ticket classification to tickets will significantly improve problem management's data mining and trending of issues.

Enterprise reporting - Applying accurate and specific ticket classification to tickets is an important prerequisite for mature enterprise reporting. Having organized support tickets will enable running reports based on issue type. You will also be able to run reports on IT services impacted and customer attributes. Reporting is critical for leadership to make business decisions. Accurate reporting is needed to measure performance and continuously improve.

Agent training – Support ticket classification can help pinpoint team and individual training needs. For example, a report can be generated to display the metrics of first contact resolution (FCR) for all tickets by agent or team. Specific ticket classifications that have low FCR percentages can be further analyzed for improvement recommendations. Management then can focus on specific IT services and provide the agent or team with better support training.

Benefits of Ticket Classification

We discussed the reasons why we organize support tickets and high-level benefits. Remember, the high-level benefits we discussed are the following.

- Cost savings
- Improved incident resolution
- Major Incident Management
- Issue avoidance
- Enterprise reporting
- Agent training

Most Help Desk managers understand that ticket classification is a powerful tool to keep issues organized. However, not all managers understand that Help Desk ticket categories are a prerequisite for many of the processes and tools the Help Desk needs. It's not enough to have Help Desk ticket categories. Help Desk ticket categories must be updated, revised, and verified to be accurate on a routine schedule.

While there are many benefits of a ticket classification project, it can be resource-intensive to complete. This ticket classification chapter will do a deeper dive into the specific benefits of ticket classification. This information helps you build a business case to justify resource time and cost. This information will also allow you to create a project scope that will include output updates to dependent processes. So, what are the specific benefits?

Cost Savings Benefit

Procurement costs – The hardware and software procurement lifecycle will be significantly improved by capturing incident and service request trends by classification types. By capturing incident data into support tickets and classifying them, you can isolate hardware and software with the highest incident occurrence. This can be very helpful for identifying the root cause. It can also be helpful in identifying specific products to avoid purchasing in the future. For example, if you have purchased two models of laptops and find one of the models has a high failure rate. The hardware, procurement, and legal managers can pursue refunds or warranty work. In addition, when it is time to purchase more laptops, you can avoid the model with a high failure rate.

Staffing costs – Generally, the largest line item in a Help Desk budget is staffing cost. The larger the staff size, the larger your budget is. What if you implement a process where agents spend less time on an individual call allowing them to handle more calls? Implementing a new ticket classification scheme is that process. It can significantly reduce the agent's average handle time (AHT) of support calls with customers. This reduction in AHT is achieved by resolving a customer's issue in a shorter period of handle time. In this guide, we will discuss how a ticket classification scheme can improve resolution time. By resolving a customer's issue quicker, the agent can then answer the next call waiting sooner. As we show in figure 3.1, increased productivity will decrease the cost per call.

AHT	Calls handled per hour	Hourly wage	Cost per call
10 minutes	6	$15	$2.50
6 minutes	10	$15	$1.50

Figure 3.1

This greater productivity in handling customer support calls will lead to efficiency adjustments of staffing levels or schedules. This does not necessarily mean you will let agents go but can eliminate future backfills or allow you to make schedule adjustments.

Reduced escalation costs – Providing a resolution to customers' issues are not completed by the Help Desk alone. Let's say 40 percent of all customer issues are currently escalated to second-level support, engineers, and developers. That means your average first contact resolution (FCR) is 60 percent. What if you improved your FCR to 80 percent? Improving FCR has two main benefits.

The first main benefit is that customer satisfaction increases when their issue is resolved on the first contact. Customers can become dissatisfied if their call is transferred. Customers also become dissatisfied if they are told an engineer will call them back when they become available. The second main benefit of an improved FCR rate is the ability to reduce escalation costs by solving more calls with lower-paid first-level support staff. This will free more expensive resources like engineers and developers to complete project work. Figure 3.2 highlights how an issue's cost increases as more expensive resources must be engaged. Issue A is resolved in 10 minutes by the Help Desk at a staffing cost of $2.50. Issue B is resolved at the second level at a combined staffing cost of $6.67. Issue C is escalated to the second level and then to an engineer or developer and finally resolved at a combined staffing cost of $12.50. In our example, we see it is 2.5 to 5 times more expensive to resolve an escalated issue versus solving it at first-level support.

Issue	Help Desk Agent ($15 hr.)	Second Level ($25 hr.)	Engineer/ Developer ($35 hr.)	Resolution cost
A	10 min.			$2.50
B	10 min.	10 min.		$6.67
C	10 min.	10 min.	10 min.	$12.50

Figure 3.2

An improved ticket classification scheme will enable you to resolve more issues at first-level support and avoid the extra costs of escalation.

Improved incident resolution

A new ticket classification scheme will improve incident resolution. Once you design and implement your new ticket classification scheme, many incident resolution processes can be leveraged more effectively. Not only will you see an improvement in incident resolution, but you will reduce staffing and escalation costs. These improvements are made possible by the following resolution support processes.

Just-in-Time knowledge – Your ticketing application can leverage your new ticket classification scheme to present just-in-time knowledge base articles. These knowledge base articles can be selected based on the ticket classification assigned, as shown in figure 3.3. For example, if your ticket is classified as a question about guest wireless or Wi-Fi, your ticketing application can present specific knowledge articles on how to help the customer set up guest wireless or Wi-Fi. How does this work?

The simplest way to explain this is your knowledge articles can be tagged with metadata that corresponds with your ticket classification scheme. When you classify a ticket with question/Wi-Fi/setup, for example, your ticket application can query and display the knowledge database for articles related to Wi-Fi setup.

Support Ticket #12345	
Tier 1	Question
Tier 2	Wi-Fi network
Tier 3	Setup

Figure 3.3

Most ticketing applications will allow the configuration of the search results based on ticket classification. In this example, the query would be based on a tier 2 Wi-Fi network and tier 3 setup. In addition, detailed criteria such as customer location, most viewed, highest rated, and last used can further filter the articles presented. If the article does provide the correct resolution solution, the article can be linked to the support ticket. This will associate the support ticket and the article for future assistance, such as the ticket matching process.

Ticket Matching – Ticket classification allows newly created tickets to be matched with previously resolved tickets with similar classification. Most ticketing applications can perform a search to present a list of resolved tickets based on ticket classification keywords. If previously resolved matching tickets use a specific knowledge article, you may be able to use the associated article link discussed in the just-in-time knowledge process. The ticket matching process is a powerful tool for a Help Desk agent to research and apply the same resolution steps used previously. Ticket matching can significantly improve First Contact Resolution (FCR) and reduce call handle time.

Decision tree scripts – When issues are more complex or could have multiple solutions to solve the issue, your Help Desk may need help troubleshooting the issue. Troubleshooting some issues can take a great deal of time. Many Help Desks will reduce the troubleshooting resolution time by offering the agents a decision tree. A decision tree presents questions with answer selections for symptoms or attributes of the customer's issue. When selecting the matching answer, the decision tree script will continue to narrow down the issue by asking additional questions. This will continue until, ultimately, a potential solution is presented. This is like the twenty questions game and is very helpful. However, creating one decision tree script for all issues would result in a huge complex decision tree. By creating smaller decision tree scripts with the starting point based on ticket classification, Help Desk Agents are more successful in finding the solution at a faster rate.

Ticket Assignment – When your Help Desk agent cannot solve an issue on the first contact, ticket classification can be used to identify which resolver group should receive the ticket assignment quickly. Rules can be set up in most ticket applications, which will associate specific ticket categories to resolver groups. Proper assignment to resolver groups will reduce ticket passing. The ticket passing process is when a ticket is incorrectly assigned to a resolver group and then must be reassigned to a different resolver group. When ticket passing occurs one or more times, precious minutes, hours, and days in delays can occur.

Major Incident Management handling

A major incident can be devastating for a company. When an IT or business service is unavailable, the loss of revenue can be enormous. User productivity can also be severely degraded. Improving the speed of detecting the major incident can reduce the overall outage duration. A ticket classification scheme is a great way to detect if the users are experiencing a widespread issue. This is called incident trending or trending of issue.

Incident Trending – For incident trending to work, a properly implemented ticket classification scheme is critical. Incident trending is where more than one incident in a short period of time has been assigned the same ticket classification. These trends feed into service monitoring tools, executive dashboards, and accurate operations reporting. By feeding the reporting tool with real-time ticket data based on the ticket classification scheme, management will be able to spot issue trends. This can speed up identifying outages, degraded IT services, and other business-impacting faults.

Incident priority - In an ideal world, when a user calls the Help Desk about a question or issue, the Help Desk agent works on the issue until resolved before starting another one. At the end of each workday in this ideal world, all customer issues are resolved, and the work queue is empty ready for the next business day. In the real world, Help Desk management realizes that a Help Desk agent's workload may be made up of dozens of open tickets carried over for days or weeks. Help Desk management also has limited funding to increase staffing levels to work on issues sequentially until resolved. Not all issues have the same impact and urgency on the business. Help Desk management must assign work based on priority. A ticket classification scheme is a valuable tool to help set the correct priority for your organization.

With the priority set correctly, the Help Desk can cost-effectively handle tickets based on that priority. By knowing what type of issue the ticket was created for, Help Desk management can ensure a resource with the correct skill-set is engaged to resolve the ticket. Ticket classification will also identify issue trends, widespread degraded service, and service outages.

Ticket classification is the primary tool for Help Desk agents to set a correct ticket priority level. High priority tickets can be quickly identified by using the new classification scheme. When the Help Desk agent applies a classification to a ticket that is associated with a mission-critical service, the ticket priority can be manually or via scripting raised to a higher priority incident. Ticket priority levels are a matrix of impact and urgency. The impact is how much it affects the business, and urgency is how quickly the business needs to have it resolved. By setting priorities to tickets, resources can focus on the most urgent issues with the largest impact on the business first. A ticket classification scheme can be used to put more weight on mission-critical services to ensure the Help Desk Agent assigns the correct priority.

Issue Avoidance

The best incident resolution is to fix the issue before the customer is impacted. This is what issue avoidance is. Much of the process for avoiding future incidents are handled through the problem management process. However, a good ticket classification scheme is a necessary input for problem management. Ticket classification of incident tickets provides a wealth of information.

Known Error Database – When a problem has been defined, it can be called a known error. A known error is a problem where the root cause has been identified and a workaround is in place. A workaround is when a full resolution is not yet available for an incident or problem, but something can be done to allow the user to complete their task. It can be very useful to display known errors based on your ticket classification. If your Help Desk Agent is presented with known errors upon assigning a ticket classification to an issue, your Help Desk Agent can easily apply the workaround or solution presented. Implementing a workaround will allow users to continue to work at some level while a permanent solution to the problem is being developed.

Event monitoring - Basic monitoring is comprised of watching for spikes in system resources such as CPU utilization, memory use, and network response. As your event monitoring becomes more advanced, your monitoring will focus on business transactions to discover and correct issues before they significantly affect your users. As events occur, your monitoring system will generate incident tickets for the impacted CI based on data drive rules. A mature IT support organization will identify a high percentage of issues by event monitoring and support teams' versus those reported by end-users.

Enterprise reporting

Ultimately to assist management with enterprise reporting, ticket classification is a necessary process. Data from Help Desk support tickets are needed as input to build reports. With this information, dozens of effective reports can be generated to give a pulse of your customer support operations. These reports can identify issue trends, training needed, purchasing decisions, and important information about the organizational structure. Below we list a few of the baseline reports that can be generated from your support data.

IT service performance – A useful report using ticket data is the number of issues reported and grouped by IT service. The source of this type of report is ticket data using the ticket classification to determine the IT service impacted.

Agent performance data – Ticket data is used to measure agent performance. Some of the performance data are first contact resolution rate and total resolution time.

Organizational data – Ticket classification data can be used to report on organizational resources. The data can quantify the use of escalation resources, such as developers and engineers. The data can also quantify the amount of Help Desk resource time consumed by IT service. This will provide developers with a wealth of information on which IT service products need improvements. New employee onboarding issues can be measured, and improvements to the new employee programs improved. You can run reports on which departments are consuming the most Help Desk resources by reporting issues or asking questions. With this report, you can work with department leaders, supervisors, and trainers to put future mitigation plans in place. Also, this resource consumption data can be used for cost chargeback. One goal of reporting using ticket data is to help the departments with their technology use and reduce the future resource consumption of your Help Desk resources.

Agent Training

Businesses are constantly making changes to IT services. New applications are implemented. Legacy applications receive updates. With all these changes to IT services, the Help Desk is the place where users will go to ask questions and report issues. It is important to document those questions and issues in support tickets. By running reports on the support ticket repository, you can find out which IT services are receiving the most questions and issues.

Reviewing questions and issues by ticket classification type will drive more effective training programs. These training programs can be for users on how to use specific functions. The training programs can also be for Help Desk agents to focus on how they can provide more effective first-level support for the IT service being reviewed. Help Desk training programs do rely on an effective ticket classification scheme. There are many inputs to the training programs. We will discuss how ticket classification impacts the following training areas.

New hire onboarding training
Ongoing training and skill development
New process training
Just in time / CBT training

New Hire Onboarding Training - It is important that the first impression of the new employee of your company is positive. Proper onboarding will improve their initial engagement and integration into their position. A new hire onboarding training program should include the following topics related to ticket classification.

A checklist and review of support ticket best practices, ticket creation, and ticket classification processes should be included.
In-depth coverage of the major IT systems, including identification of mission-critical IT systems, should be discussed.
An in-depth review of the ticket escalation process, escalation groups, and key personnel should be part of the training.
Incident prioritization processes and how to engage the incident management team are important topics.

Ongoing training and skill development - An ongoing training program is important for employees to refresh their current required knowledge of work practices. This includes using your new ticket classification scheme. Ongoing training will also assist employees by incrementally improving their skills. Companies will use ongoing training to keep up with industry changes and the latest technology to stay ahead of competitors. This training will also reduce skill gaps and allow employees to meet the requirements of their job description.

New process and application training - When things change at a company, employees need to have the training to succeed. When a company implements a new complex process or if a new enterprise application is to be introduced, specific training may be needed. The training should cover how to support the new process and application. The training should identify when the new process and application will be implemented. If the new process and application have issues beyond what the Help Desk can support, the training should identify how to escalate the issue for assistance.

The ticket classification process is critical when introducing a new process and application. The new process and application training should cover new classification terms and tiers added or removed from the ticket classification scheme. Frequently when a new term or new tier structure is added, there is a percentage of agents that either don't know or understand their use. Proper training should reduce this confusion. In addition, new knowledge base articles, decision trees, and ticket matching tools should be reviewed in the new process and application training.

Just in time / CBT training - Sometimes, employees will not internalize the information until a later time when they actually have to use it. Just in time and CBT training is a good option to provide on-the-spot training when an employee is confronted with a new process and application. This training could be provided by an in-person visit by a trainer, a computer-based training video, or a quick reference card at the employee's work location

Ticket Classification Worksheet

This ticket classification worksheet gives your ticket classification project team a summary of the major steps to complete a ticket classification project successfully.

Step 1 - Start by enforcing support ticket best practices.

Every Help Desk will have processes on how to create and handle support tickets. For your new ticket classification to work well, your ticket data needs to be consistent and follow best practices.

Support tickets are mandatory – Treat support tickets as an official record. For all support interactions, a ticket documenting the support provided must be created.

Ticket documentation must be descriptive – The support ticket documentation must be detailed and descriptive. Ticketing documentation must capture who, what, when, where, and how.

Ticket comments should identify the contributor – As information is added to the support ticket, it is important to know who added the information. Each ticket comment should be associated with the contributor of the comment. This provides an audit trail to the historical record.

No ambiguous classification terms – The ticket classification scheme should not include ambiguous terms such as other, miscellaneous, and issue.

Step 2 - Build your ticket classification project team.

The Help Desk cannot complete the ticket classification project successfully without assistance. It is important that the following experts are part of the project team.

Ticketing Application Administrator/Developer – The incident and service request form in your ticketing application may need to be modified. These experts will be responsible for adjusting configurations and implementing field modifications as needed.

Help Desk Manager/staff – Not only are the Help Desk manager and staff stakeholders, but they should be part of the project team.

Application Owners / Resolver Groups – Escalated support tickets are typically handled by resolver groups outside the Help Desk. Ensure application owners and resolver groups are part of the project team to ensure success.

Knowledgebase Manager – The knowledge base will need to be updated as part of the ticket classification project. To be successful, ensure representatives from the knowledge base team are part of the project.

Reporting Manager – Changes to the ticket classification fields, terms, and structure will require coordination with the reporting team to update the report source links.

Problem Manager – Changes to the ticket classification scheme will have an impact on problem management activities.

Voice of the Customer – If your company uses a self-service portal or other customer-facing processes, it is important to have the representation of customer-focused representatives.

Step 3 - Legacy ticket data collection

Six months of legacy ticket data should be queried and exported. The following ticket data fields should be exported into a spreadsheet.

Ticket number – The ticket number will be the unique key to allow you to review the complete ticket record from the ticketing application as needed.

Classification data – Exporting the legacy ticket classification field data (tier 1, tier 2, tier 3) is important. Include columns and fields for this data.

Ticket summary – Exporting the ticket summary can assist the project team in designing what the new ticket category should be.

Ticket detail – The ticket detail can really provide insight into what the issue is and assist with creating new terms.

Ticket creation date – To understand the frequency of term use, you will need a creation date to run some trending reports.

Ticket resolution summary/resolution code – The resolution summary or resolution code will provide detail of what the issue truly was and how it was resolved.

Agent Name – Exporting the agent name will allow the project team the ability to review tickets with the creator of the ticket.

Escalation group – Being able to search, sort, and group tickets by escalation groups can offer a lot of insight into ticket data.

Step 4 - Legacy ticket data review

Legacy ticket data holds a wealth of useful historical support data. Using legacy ticket data will reduce ticket classification assumptions and will help the project team create the future state ticket classification scheme.

Add future state columns – Add the future state columns to the exported data spreadsheet. These future state columns will hold the proposed terms for the new tier structure.

Add a notes column - An additional column that may be added is a notes column. This will allow the project team to add notes during the legacy ticket date review process.

Highlight data rows requiring action - Creating a color-coded highlight system will identify the specific actions needed at the end of the review.

Group by ticket classification categories. Create a pivot table to display the most and seldom-used legacy ticket categories.

Overused categories - Identify over-used legacy ticket categories, which could be candidates to break up.

Underused categories - Identify seldom used legacy ticket categories and consolidate them with other similar categories.

Isolated incident driving events – Sometimes, an isolated event such as a data center power outage will create a large volume of incidents in a short period of time. You need to disposition how this historical trend may impact the legacy category use analysis.

Eliminate ambiguous categories - Identify and replace ambiguous categories such as other, miscellaneous, and issue with an appropriate category.

Document and fix weaknesses – While you are reviewing the ticket data, you will see many areas of weakness with the ticket data, such as poorly documented titles, descriptions, and summaries. All these issues need to be documented for future agent guidance and training sessions.

Step 5 - Create a future state ticket classification scheme.

While reviewing the legacy ticket classification scheme and ticket data, the project team will start to form ideas for the new scheme. Below are three frequent ticket classification schemes for your consideration.

Ticket Classification Scheme 1 – By ticket type

This ticket classification scheme is based on grouping tickets by what type of ticket is being created. Below are some of the major ticket types.

Incident – An incident is an unplanned interruption or quality reduction to an IT service. The incident ticket type is used when the customer reports that something is broken.

Service request – A Service Request is a process for your Help Desk customers to request system access, information, or a standard low-risk change to be fulfilled. A service request ticket type is used when the customer is requesting something.

Question – The question ticket type is used when the customer is asking a "how do I" question.

Tier structure by ticket type

If you choose a new ticket classification scheme using the ticket type, we have the following suggested keywords.

Tier 1 – Ticket types - such as Incident, Service Request, and questions.

Tier 2 – Service - such as Telecom, Mobile Device, and Infrastructure. These are the high-level IT services you may see on department or leadership reports for the enterprise or business.

Tier 3 – Product name - such as Avaya phone, iPhone, or SharePoint. The product name is the configuration item that makes up the IT service and is the focus of the incident or service request.

Advantages

This scheme identifies ticket types in tier 1 is helpful if the ticketing application does not have a way of separating ticket types.

With this scheme, you are able to distinguish assistance for broken items. You are also able to identify a request for new services and customer questions.

Service Level management SLAs and OLAs can be applied at the root level.

Able to run reports based on IT services for reporting and improvement efforts.

Disadvantages

Using a ticket type term for the tier 1 field will reduce the available tiers to create a more detailed ticket classification scheme.

Tier 2 categories can be very repetitive. You may have to have the same tier 2 terms under each of the tier 1 terms.

This scheme does not include a tier for a verb or action word such as repaired, reset, or installed.

Ticket Classification Scheme 2 – By IT Service

The second ticket classification scheme template to discuss is by IT service. This ticket classification scheme is based on grouping tickets by what IT service where support is being provided.

Tier structure by IT service – If you choose a new ticket classification scheme using IT service, we have the following suggested keywords.

Tier 1 – IT Services - such as Telecom, Mobile Device, and Printing. These are the high-level IT services you may see on department or leadership reports for the enterprise or business.

Tier 2 – Action – Verb of action needed such as configure, restart, and unlock.

Tier 3 – Product names - such as Jabber, bulk printing, and password.

Advantages

This scheme organizes tickets by IT services in the tier 1 field. This type of tier structure works well for creating reports by enterprise IT services. It also works well for quickly determining what the escalation group is that supports the IT service.

The tier 2 field is a verb and clearly identifies what action was taken in the ticket to resolve.

The tier 3 field is the product name, which will help identify the specific component of the tier 1 IT service that support was provided.

Disadvantages

Having too many verbs to choose from in tier 2 can lead to a lot of product name repetition in tier 3.

Tier 3 product name field could be unnecessary in the organization depending on the use of a configuration/asset database.

Ticket Classification Scheme 3 – By department, line of business, or company.

This ticket classification scheme is based on grouping tickets by what department, line of business, or company the customer reporting the issue.

Tier structure by the department, line of business, or company

If you choose a new ticket classification scheme using department, line of business, or company, we have the following suggested keywords.

Tier 1 – Department, line of business or company - such as accounting, marketing, and sales department. Sometimes tier 1 terms can include the line of business or a company.

Tier 2 – IT Service - such as Telecom, Mobile Device, and Printing. These are the high-level IT services you may see on reports for the department, line of business, or company.

Tier 3 – Action – Verb of action needed such as configure, restart, and unlock.

Advantages

Including department, business, or company name in the tier 1 field is a great benefit when tickets are escalated to SMEs and developers in that department, line of business, or company.

This ticket classification scheme simplifies metric reporting to the department, line of business, or company management.

This ticket classification scheme is a budget-friendly structure for ticket cost chargeback to the department, line of business, or company.

Disadvantages

This may lead to classification confusion for organizations with many cross-functional teams.

Using a department or company name as a tier 1 category may force a future classification scheme. If the organization changes its department or company name, the classification structure must be updated.

Step 6 - Apply the future state classification scheme to evaluate

Reclassifying the legacy exported ticket data with the future state classification scheme will make clear where the gaps are.

Select a ticket classification scheme type - Choose a ticket classification scheme to use for your future state. You can use one of the examples previously described or your own variation.

Create a tiered matrix of classification terms - Before adding the ticket classification terms to your legacy ticket data spreadsheet, it is advised to create a tiered matrix of classification terms. This matrix is a brainstorming session of the likely terms that will be used in each of the tiers.

Apply the selected ticket classification scheme to the legacy ticket data - Once you complete this matrix, you can reference this when selecting terms to apply to the legacy ticket data for evaluation. Go through the entire six months of legacy ticket data in your spreadsheet and apply the new ticket classification scheme.
Most frequent problems identified.

Missing classification terms – There will be tickets where there is not a classification from the future state classification scheme matrix that accurately fits with some tickets.

Conflicting classification terms – The team may find two or more classifications from the future state classification scheme matrix, which could apply to a ticket.

Step 7 - Ensure ticket classification category balance.

The adjusting step is a very important review process for your ticket classification project. The goal of this adjustment is to ensure the future state classification scheme is well balanced.

Overpopulated classifications – Ticket classification is less effective if too many tickets are classified under the same term. Identify and break up overpopulated categories into smaller and more specific terms.

Underpopulated classifications – If you have too many classification terms to select from, it will take longer to classify tickets. If you have underpopulated ticket buckets, you should consider merging these into relevant categories together.

Creating reports – When changes are made to the ticket classification scheme, reports that use the ticket data as a source can have errors. Make sure that the reports run, and they can use the new classification scheme correctly.

Resolution support tools – The Help Desk can have tools available that assist the agent in finding a resolution to issues. Testing of these tools must happen to ensure they work correctly with the new ticket classification scheme.

Step 8 - Ensure the support staff are trained

Training is critical to ensure the support staff understands the new Help Desk ticket classification scheme.

Communication – Setting the expectation that the ticket classification scheme is being positively updated is important. It is important to communicate a summary of the changes and the timing of the changes.

Test environment training – We recommend that Help Desk agents receive access to this test environment that has the new classification structure implemented.

Create quick reference charts – It is recommended to have quick reference charts available at each Help Desk agent workspace. The agents will need the ability to refer to the quick reference charts as needed.

Discuss the "review needed" term – Train the support staff that selecting the "review needed" keywords in the ticket classification will engage a management review. During the management review, it will be determined if a new term is needed

Step 9 - Implement the ticket classification scheme into the production

Now it's time to execute the implementation plan. The implementation plan for the new ticket classification scheme involves a few steps.

Understand the process – Changing the ticket classification scheme and updating legacy ticket data may take some time and effort. Make sure you understand the implementation process. Determine if there will be any ticketing application downtime and ensure you have developed a valid backout plan.

New ticket creation - It is recommended to execute the implementation during evenings or weekends to minimize disruptions to the agents. Agents may need a manual process to document support efforts during this downtime and then create the tickets once the ticketing application is available again.

Legacy ticket classification – After the new ticket classification scheme is implemented for new ticket creation, the legacy support ticket should be updated with the new scheme. By updating historical ticket data for at least one year back, you will be able to run reports, perform trends, and facilitate customer history lookup.

Respond to issues - Moving the ticket classification scheme into production may uncover issues that should be addressed. During the execution step, feedback is critical for continuous improvement. To allow users of the ticketing application the ability to provide feedback and report issues, you need a reporting process. Using the "review needed" classification may be the best way of tracking and resolving issues quickly.

Missing terms – If the users identify a missing term, there should be a formal request for the review process to suggest a new term.

Chapter 18

Design a Call Volume Management Strategy

Chapter Objectives

- Learn why you should use Help Desk call volume management strategies.
- Understand what the most common use call volume management strategies used are.
- Review customer call metrics.

When you read the chapter titled Help Desk call volume management strategies, you may be thinking this is about work avoiding schemes agents use to avoid taking calls. While Help Desk agents trying to avoid calls is an important performance management issue to discuss, this chapter will be focused on how to reduce or spread-out inbound call volume. Help Desk managers will employ call volume management strategies to reduce the number of live assisted calls. They will also use these strategies to spread out the calls to a more manageable pattern.

Why use Help Desk call volume management strategies?

Help Desk managers will employ call volume management strategies to optimize the workforce, reduce costs, and improve customer satisfaction. Let's explore these reasons in more detail.

Workforce Management

Staffing live support 24x7 can be very difficult. A normal workweek for agents is 8 hours a day for five days a week. 20 to 30% of that time is away from the phone for training, breaks, and other activities. In addition, agents have time off allowances for vacations and sick time. There are 168 work hours in a seven-day calendar week. Trying to assure there is at least one agent available to answer a call can be challenging. To allow for time off the phones and time away, you really need to staff at least two agents per shift. Even using flexible scheduling techniques, you will need at least ten agents.

Increasing staffing levels may also be needed to meet the high-volume periods. These increased staffing levels can further drive up labor costs and lead to excess labor capacity return to a low call volume period. For example, Monday mornings are typically a high call volume period. In contrast, Friday morning can be significantly different. If you staff up to handle the high periods for things like password resets, what do you do with the excess labor capacity during slow periods?

Cost containment

Staffing live support, especially 24x7, can be very expensive. Live Help Desk support can be one of the most expensive forms of support offered. For example, a very routine support call is a password reset. Let's say a password reset can be completed in 7 minutes, and an agent makes $20 per hour. That means the call cost $2.34 for staffing to handle the password reset. What if you could use self-service technology to avoid the call? Most likely, you will reduce your cost and change call volume patterns.

Customer satisfaction

One-factor impacting customer satisfaction scores are long periods of hold time. Customers hate waiting on hold for the next available agent. Many customers also would rather use self-service tools instead of calling the Help Desk. Reducing the hold time and providing self-service tools could significantly improve customer satisfaction.

What are the most common use call volume management strategies used?

Help Desk Managers use many call avoidance strategies to reduce live assisted call volume, reduce peak volume calls, and ultimately reduce staffing costs. Call avoidance strategies include the following:

Use Self Service Password Resets

One of the highest call volume and cost drivers is password-related calls. Users forget their passwords over weekends, especially during holiday weeks. To compound the problem, Information Security is enforcing complex password requirements. Many companies do not allow repeat passwords and require special characters. Customers manage their passwords with self-service password reset tools. Self-service password reset tools will give customers the ability to unlock, reset, and change passwords without calling the Help Desk.

Front-end message

A front-end message is a recorded message informing the caller of specific information. Typically, this message will provide the customer with a notice that there is an ongoing incident causing a widespread user-impacting issue. During a widespread issue, the Help Desk will receive more calls than they can handle. When a customer calls the Help Desk, they usually are presented with a greeting and a menu of selections for the type of support they are seeking. Finally, if a Help

Desk agent is not immediately available to handle the call, the customer is placed into a queue to wait for the next available agent. The greeting can be appended with a front-end message. The goal of a front-end message is to inform the customer there is an issue, give them any available workaround information and ultimately hang up to reduce the volume of calls agents must handle.

Automated customer return call

This is a service that will ask the customer if they would like to avoid waiting and have a Help Desk agent call them back when they are available. A customer call-back service has several benefits. First, the customer will avoid becoming upset about the long wait time. Second, this will smooth out the call pattern and avoid many callers waiting in the queue. Overall, a customer call-back service may lower your abandonment rate and improve customer satisfaction.

Overflow assistance

Sometimes, even with your best efforts at scheduling enough resources and employing other call volume management strategies, you need more people answering calls. Training overflow resources may help. An overflow resource could be desktop support technicians, trainers, and software engineers. These resources can be set up in an overflow queue. When call volume reaches a point where there are no available agents and the wait time for callers breaches a threshold, calls can be routed to the overflow queue.

Improve user training

A large driver of Help Desk call volume can be attributed to changes in the IT services environment. If a change is being planned for an IT service, providing end-users pre-change training may avoid calls. One example of a change that could use end-user training is implementing a new application or installing a new module. This new IT service training could include how to log in, review what is changing, and let users ask questions. Providing chair drops and a web page with frequently asked questions about the new IT service could also be helpful.

Help Desk managers seeking to optimize the workforce, reduce costs, and improve customer satisfaction should focus on call volume management processes. By implementing some of the suggestions we made, the benefits realized will be significant.

Call Volume Management Worksheet

As we stated in the chapter, Help Desk managers will employ call volume management strategies to optimize the workforce, reduce costs, and improve customer satisfaction. There are many off-the-shelf applications, services, and solutions available to implement and can save money overall. Here are our recommendations.

Step 1 – Take a snapshot of the current costs, issue types, and call volume state.

Throughout this book, we explain how to gather call data such as cost per ticket, issue category type, and call volume. Taking a snapshot of the current costs, issue types, and call volume will give you a good starting baseline. This will allow you to use this baseline data to see if you are improving as you implement improvements.

Step 2 – Implement a self-service password management system.

Self-service password management systems have been around for a long time. Every phone system and ticket application has APIs to allow the self-service password management system to integrate seamlessly. Self-service password reset tools will give customers the ability to unlock, reset, and change passwords without calling the Help Desk. Self-service password reset tools can significantly reduce costs and call volumes. To implement a self-service password management system, follow these steps.

1. **Gather the password management activity data.** The activity data includes the volume of calls and tickets. The activity data includes the average duration of the calls and cost

per call. The goal is to determine how much time and money your Help Desk is spending on password management.
2. **Research the current top password management systems available.** I did not include specific names in this book due to how fast technology changes.
3. **Create a finalist list.** Setup three password management vendors to provide a demonstration and a quote for their system.
4. **Select and implement the self-service password management system.** Once implemented, you should find a reduction in call flows to the Help Desk. This should improve metrics and allow you to adjust staffing levels to save money.

Step 3 – Implement front-end messages during events and outages.

A front-end message is a recorded message informing the caller of specific information. Typically, this message will provide the customer with a notice that there is an ongoing incident causing a widespread user-impacting issue. The goal of a front-end message is to inform the customer there is an issue, give them any available workaround information and ultimately hang up to reduce the volume of calls agents must handle. To get started.

- Ensure your phone system ACD allows front-end messages. If not, speak to your phone support team or vendor to enable it.
- Create a couple of front-end message templates. Even writing down a generic script will help. The last thing you want to do is try and create a front-end message from scratch during an event or outage.
- Create a procedure and train your staff on how and when to use front-end messages.

Step 4 – Implement automatic customer call-back service

A customer call-back service will ask the customer if they would like to avoid waiting and have a Help Desk agent call them back when they are available. Overall, a customer call-back service may lower your abandonment rate and improve customer satisfaction. To get started.
- Ensure your phone system ACD allows customer call-backs. If not, speak to your phone support team or vendor to enable it.
- Create a procedure and train your staff on how the customer call-back service works and what is expected of them.

Step 5 – Implement overflow assistance.

When call volume reaches a point where there are no available agents and the wait time for callers breaches a threshold, calls can be routed to the overflow assistance queue. To get started.
- Identify the resources that would be part of the overflow assistance queue. This could be the desktop support staff, network engineers, and other IT staff in the department.
- Create the call flow logic in your ACD for the overflow assistance queue and assign the members.
- Train the staff on when overflow assistance would be used and how it will work. This includes training the staff on how to log into and out of the overflow assistance queue.

Chapter 19

Implement a Shift-Left Support Strategy

Chapter Objectives

- Learn the benefits of having a shift left support strategy.
- Understand how a shift left support strategy can save the IT department a lot of money.
- Understand how a shift left support strategy can make your IT Engineers more productive.

An enormously powerful strategy for making your Help Desk cost-effective and reducing the burden of repetitive work on your IT engineers is a shift-left support strategy. Implementing a shift-left support strategy has become popular in the IT service management community. A shift-left support strategy is based on moving service and support requests from high-cost support engineers and developers to lower-cost tier 1 Help Desk agents. Even better, the shift-left support strategy can also move the work further left by empowering customers to fulfill their needs using self-service tools. By moving work to the left, it will reduce overall cost and free up the time of your

IT engineers to work on more productive work. Let us look at how we use our IT engineer's time more effectively.

Using IT Engineer's time effectively

The Help Desk is great at resolving routine and well-documented issues. The Help Desk also has established troubleshooting methods that can lead to resolving some more complex issues. If a customer is having a unique or seemingly complex issue, the Help Desk may not be equipped to resolve the issue. If the Help Desk is not able to resolve an issue or fulfill a request, they update the support ticket with the support steps already tried. The ticket is then escalated to the next level of support. In most cases, the next level of support is an IT engineering or application support team.

IT Engineers and application support personnel are great at solving problems. IT engineers will work with developers, SMEs, and the vendor to solve it. This is a beautiful process to watch. All this talent and brainpower come to bear on solving the customer's issue. Once the issue is known, the IT engineers will devise a plan to resolve the issue. The resolution could spin off a change to eliminate the defect from the environment. The resolution could be implementing a workaround to get the customer up and running. Also, the resolution may just be actions that require the IT engineer's advanced knowledge or access. When the customer's issue is ultimately resolved, the ticket is sent back to the Help Desk to confirm the closure with the customer. To this point, the process worked well. However, what if the issue occurs with other customers?

Solving problems versus a redundant task

When the same issue repeatedly comes into the Help Desk and is ultimately escalated to the IT engineer's support ticket queue, this issue turns into a redundant task. Is working on this known issue the best use of their talent and time of your expensive resources? The IT engineer has already come up with a resolution for the issue. They already know how to resolve the problem. Their valuable and expensive time should be focused on more complex tasks and projects. For some companies, they will remain at this level of maturity. The same issues will be passed from the Help Desk to IT engineering over and over. Our goal is to devise a plan to stop this process and put a better plan in place.

In our shift-left support strategy, we want to move the support of these known repetitive issues to lower-tier support like a Help Desk agent. To do this, it will require effort from the IT engineer and others to determine what is needed by the Help Desk to resolve these issues. Once a support plan is devised, the IT engineer will document the support into the knowledgebase. The Help Desk agent then can follow the knowledgebase article and resolve the issue without engaging IT engineers and developers. This will free the IT engineer and developer's time to work on other higher-priority issues and projects.

Cost-effective support

We discussed how the shift-left support strategy could free IT engineers and developers time to work on higher priority issues and projects. This sounds great, but what does this mean for overall costs? The shift-left support strategy transfers repeatable and well-documented work. The work is transferred from high-cost resources such as IT engineers to lower-cost resources at the Help Desk. This transfer of work does have a significant benefit to the overall IT department budget. How? Let's look at the following example.

A customer calls the Help Desk with an issue. The Help Desk agent troubleshoots the issue for fifteen minutes. After fifteen minutes, the Help Desk agent determines they don't have the knowledge or access to resolve the issue. The caller is told the issue must be escalated to an IT engineer. The Help Desk agent takes another five minutes to document the details of the call and issue. The Help Desk agent has spent a total of twenty minutes on an issue and has not been able to resolve it. The customer is still having an issue and is waiting.

Cost so far

Help Desk agent – 20 min X $18 per hour = $6.12

Later that day, the issue ticket is then assigned to an IT engineer. The engineer spends five minutes reading the notes. The engineer then calls the user and then spends another fifteen minutes working on the issue. Once the engineer is able to resolve the issue, he takes another five minutes to document the work. The engineer then sends the resolved ticket back to the Help Desk.

Cost so far

Help Desk agent – 20 min X $18 per hour = $6.12

IT engineer – 25 min X $40 = $16.66

The Help Desk agent receives the ticket back into their queue. After reading the work notes for five minutes, the Help Desk reaches out to the customer. The Help Desk agent, as the ticket owner, is required to confirm everything is working for the customer. The Help Desk agent and customer have a quick 3-minute conversation confirming the ticket can be closed.

Total ticket cost

Help Desk agent – 20 min X $18 per hour = $6.12

IT engineer – 25 min X $40 = $16.66

Help Desk agent – 7 minutes = $2.10

Total ticket cost = $24.88

The end result is if the Help Desk agent had the knowledge and access, they might have been able to resolve the customer's issue at first contact. This means the total ticket support cost could have been limited to $6.12. Since the Help Desk was not empowered to resolve the issue, the ticket cost quadrupled to $24.88. Even worse, take this cost and multiply it by 100 or 1000 tickets annually, and you have a high cost for just this specific issue. The shift-left support strategy can be used to reduce the costs of supporting these issues. It also can be used cost-effectively in supporting fulfilling service requests.

Fulfilling requests for service

In my time assisting Help Desk managers in implementing best practices, I see a pattern where the Help Desk is not empowered to process service requests to the extent that they could. One of the reasons the Help Desk cannot fulfill requests for service is system knowledge. A generalist at the Help Desk will not know applications and services with the depth that an SME, engineer, or developer would. An important way to transfer this knowledge is through knowledge articles and training sessions. By sharing this application and services information, the Help Desk agent will be better prepared to support requests for services.

Another reason the Help Desk cannot fulfill requests for service just comes down to not having proper access and permissions to fulfill the request. Some companies keep the access and control to fulfill these service requests with a small group of IT engineers. The Help Desk agent has no choice but to escalate these requests. In our shift-left support strategy, we find ways to delegate the control and knowledge safely to the Help Desk. When I use the term safely, I am referring to delegating only enough permissions to complete the work to fulfill the request and no more.

Fundamentals of the shift-left support strategy

Knowledge management – A shift-left support strategy is focused on transferring duties and processes to the Help Desk staff from desktop support, IT engineers, and developers. Creating usable knowledge articles will be critical to ensure successful implantation.

Access management – Implementing a shift-left support strategy may involve delegating elevated access to the Help Desk staff. Working with your IT security and access management groups will be critical to avoiding any unnecessary security risks. Ensure only appropriate access is delegated for the Help Desk staff to perform their new duties.

Organizational change – Implementing a support strategy like shift-left can be a disruptive but positive change to your support processes. Anytime there is a change in the way an organization does something, there can be angst, confusion, and uncertainty. With stakeholder involvement, communication, and education, we can make the adoption of a shift-left support strategy successful.

End-user self-service – The most cost-effective delivery of IT services is allowing customers to obtain what they need on their own. By offering end-user self-service tools, the cost of provisioning services can be minimal. In addition, customer satisfaction tends to improve when a customer can obtain what they need at the time they want it.

Automation – IT labor costs are a large portion of any IT support department's budget. Once end-user support and provisioning processes are set up, these processes can run without much or any labor effort. More importantly, automation can reduce the overall cost significantly.

Implement a shift-left support process

By moving work to the left, it will reduce the overall cost of your IT department. Your IT engineers will be freed up to work on more productive work. Use the shift-left support strategy worksheet to start implementing shift-left at your company today!

Implement a Shift-Left Support Strategy Worksheet

In this worksheet, we will be walking through the steps to implement a shift-left support strategy in your department.

Step 1 – Gather the ticket data.

The first step is to define the universe of incident or service request tickets that were not able to be solved or provisioned by the Help Desk. This means we want to identify the tickets that were escalated to desktop support, IT engineers, developers, and vendors. Ideally, you want to gather at least six months' worth of ticket data.

Step 2 – Filter and group the ticket data.

With at least six months of ticket data collected, we will want to filter out tickets resolved on the first contact. We then want to group the ticket data by categories. The idea is to understand what incidents and service requests are being frequently requested by customers grouped by type.

Step 3 – Sort by escalation groups.

At this point, we have gathered ticket data, filtered out the tickets resolved on the first contact, and grouped the tickets by categories. Now we want to sort the ticket data by the escalation group that solved the incident or provisioned the request. Identifying the escalation group will help us document and create a process for the Help Desk to take on this activity.

Step 4 – Prioritize the best shift-left candidates

Not every incident or service request will be a good initial candidate to shift left. With hundreds of non-FCR ticket categorized tickets, it's best to start with the groups with the best probability of success.

- It is good to start with candidates with a high volume of occurrences.
- Good candidates to also start with are candidates with little or no additional access rights needed by the Help Desk agent to process.
- Candidates that are not overly complex and can have a step-by-step process made are good candidates.

Step 5 - Meet with the escalation group managers

Now that you analyzed your ticket data and have a good list of shift-left candidates, it's time to meet with the escalation group managers. The goal of the meeting is to review the shift-left candidates with the manager of the escalation group that was able to solve the incident or request. The conversation should focus on the following.

- Review the shift-left candidate and determine if the Help Desk can handle these issues.
- Determine what additional access the Help Desk would need to handle these issues.
- Decide on which shift-left candidates will move to the Help Desk.
- Identify, with the escalation group managers, what resources are available to assist with transitioning the shift-left candidates to the Help Desk.

Step 6 – Implement the shift-left plan

Now that you have determined which shift-left candidates are moving to the Help Desk, you must prepare the Help Desk team for the new work. If you were able to obtain transition resources from the escalation group, they would be able to identify all the transition steps. In general, here are the most common transition steps.

- Identify and provide access to Help Desk staff to perform the shift-left work.
- Create a training plan and train the Help Desk staff on the shift-left work.
- Create the necessary knowledge articles, ticket categories, and escalation paths in the ticket application and knowledgebase to support this shift-left work.
- Determine a cut-over date and time. Once cut over, monitor the success and watch for issues.

Customers Section

Customers are the lifeblood of any company. In this section, we will be discussing topics about customers. First, we will discuss learning the business. To learn the business, you must understand what the mission-critical services are and what is needed to support them. You also must understand who the stakeholder groups are and what is most important to them. Another important aspect of the customer section is marketing the helpdesk. We will show you how to create a welcome guide, update your Help Desk portal and why you should hold a technology fair. We also will show you the typical customer issues you may encounter at the Help Desk. This includes how to handle the most common customer service complaints. Finally, we will talk about total contact ownership and benefits.

Chapter 20

Learn the business

> **Chapter Objectives**
>
> - Learn what the mission-critical services are at your company.
> - Identify your key stakeholders.
>   - Your boss.
>   - Your customers.
>   - Your staff.
>   - Your vendors.
> - Understand why it is important to meet with the key stakeholder groups.

The role of the Help Desk manager is focused on providing customer and business support. What if your Help Desk team has limited resources? How do you appropriately allocate support? An immature Help Desk may approach this with a first in, first out, or whoever screams the loudest approach. While this may have limited success, we need to start thinking about how to prioritize issues. Due to most Help Desk resource constraints, not all incidents can be worked on simultaneously. Incident tickets will need to be prioritized based on impact and urgency. The incident impact is the potential financial, brand, or security damage caused by the incident on the business organization before it can be resolved. Urgency is how quickly incident resolution is required.

Mission-critical services

By knowing your company's business, products, and applications, you can begin to prioritize incidents. It is important that the Help Desk understands from the business what services are mission-critical. Mission-critical services are the highest priority, and your department needs to be experts at supporting them. It is important to meet with department leaders and staff regularly. The leaders and staff can tell you what services and processes are the most important for their department to run their business. In addition, the Help Desk will need to understand the interlinking of services. One department's mission-critical service can be dependent on a service managed by another department. Since there is a dependency, both services should be treated as mission-critical.

Meet with key stakeholder groups

Careers are built on a foundation of communications and strong relationships. It is important to quickly build relationships and collaborate with key stakeholders of your support department to be successful. A new Help Desk Manager needs to have clear lines of communication with at least four key stakeholder groups. These four key stakeholder groups are your boss, the customers you support, the staff that reports to you, and your vendors. Understanding the stakeholder group's perspective of the support your department provides is very important. This perspective will tell you what is working and what is not. A stakeholder may raise an issue of something not working correctly. They most likely will not know the root cause of the issues they raise. All items raised should be logged, researched, and, if applicable, have a solution implemented. This will help you uncover real or perceived issues. Timely feedback on the status of this investigation is critical. It is important to be very familiar with the contracted services you have with your vendors. You must ensure you have processes in place to measure the vendor's performance.

Your boss

Remember, your boss also has a boss who expects solutions and results. It is critically important to understand your boss's short-term and long-term goals, objectives, and priorities. This will allow you to set your department's goals, objectives, and priorities that are in alignment. Set up a method to track your progress against completing your department's goals, objectives, and priorities. When providing updates and communicating with your boss, understanding the preferred communication method is important. Some people prefer email updates, while others like in person. It is always a good idea to include the baseline status, recap the improvements made, and then provide details of how the improvement was made to the business.

Action Steps

Key stakeholder – Your Boss

1. Meet with your boss to set your department's goals, objectives, and priorities.
2. Discuss with your boss any issues with your department.
3. Setup an agreed method to report your progress addressing issues and status against meeting your department's goals, objectives, and priorities.
4. Try to secure a reoccurring scheduled 1:1 meeting with your boss. A weekly meeting with a set agenda is preferred.

Your customers

Customers of a Help Desk can be from internal departments, external companies, or the direct public. Most of the following information is based on internal departments as your customer, but these principles can translate into external support with slight modifications. Keeping the customers happy, productive, and informed is a top priority for your department. It is your job as a leader to ensure the customer service meets or exceeds your customer's expectations. You must ensure customers receive proactive and timely communications about significant changes or outages that will impact their area. Agreeing with customers on expected levels of service is critical for success. For example, if your customer expects a new printer order to be fulfilled within three business days and your team thinks five days are reasonable, you will not meet customer expectations most of the time.

Action Steps

1. Identify your customer groups and set up introductory meetings with leaders from each group. If you have external customers, you may have an internal account or service delivery managers to meet with.
2. Have your customer identify their most important or mission-critical applications or services. If you have external customers, this information can be found by looking at ticket trends.
3. Determine how well your team is fulfilling the services by investigating your ticket metrics of Key Performance Indicators (KPIs).
4. Ask your customer what the top things are they recommend to be changed or improved. It is also important to ask what things are performing well and should not be changed.
5. With the gathered information, agree with your customer what the most critical improvement actions should have the highest priority.
6. Try to secure a reoccurring scheduled meeting with the leadership of the customer groups. A monthly meeting with a set agenda is preferred.

Your staff

Your staff is concerned with their pay, schedule, work environment, career opportunities, and recognition of their efforts. They want to feel appreciated. Otherwise, morale, productivity, and employee engagement will be negatively impacted. To keep staff engaged, you and their direct supervisor must meet with them regularly. This means meeting with staff individually and as a team. As a new manager, it is important to create positive energy in the work environment by obtaining input from the staff on what issues are present and acting on them. Many companies use an outside consultant as the initial meeting facilitator to create a safe and confidential environment. Staff will be more comfortable confiding with an outside consultant and will improve the detail and accuracy of the information gathered. Once you have the compiled input from the staff, the results should be shared and discussed with the team. The discussion should lead to recommendations to correct issues. Then meet with the department leadership to discuss issues and recommended improvements. Come up with a priority plan to implement the approved improvements. Continuously communicate the issues, improvement plan, and implementation status to the staff.

Action Steps

1. Setup reoccurring monthly team and individual contributor meetings. Weekly team meetings and monthly individual meetings are recommended.
2. For your initial meetings, compiled a list of issues and proposed solutions.
3. Secure agreement and buy-in from your boss and staff on the proposed solutions.
4. Prioritize the list of solutions, define an implementation plan, and assign projects and tasks.
5. Communicate status of your improvements with accurate metrics and data to your stakeholders.

Vendors

Vendors must be actively managed and have clear lines of communication, so it is important to be engaged. Start by reviewing the current contracted agreement between your company and vendors. Understand the who, what, when, and how specified in the contract. The agreement will have very important information specifying the service they provide and should have measurable targets identified. Analyze performance reports and determine what areas of improvement are needed, including the actual performance report data. Once you have a good understanding of the agreed service targets in the contract and performance, it is time to reach out to the vendor account manager. Have scheduled a status meeting and ensure that you receive good performance reports.

Action Steps

1. Review vendor contracts related to your department and any performance reports provided by the vendor.
2. Document any gaps in service, areas of concern, and information needed in the future.
3. Meet with the vendor account team. Discuss gaps in service, areas of concern, and information needed in the future.
4. Establish a reoccurring meeting with each vendor to discuss performance and improvement initiatives. Preferably schedule a weekly meeting.

Chapter 21

Marketing the Help Desk

> **Chapter Objectives**
>
> - Learn how to start to market the Help Desk.
>   - Help Desk general information.
>   - Welcome guide.
>   - Quick reference guides.
>   - Help Desk website/portal.
>   - Informational Roadshows.
>   - Brown bag sessions.
>   - Technology fairs.
> - Complete the Help Desk marketing worksheet.

The services offered by your Help Desk have value only if they are being consumed. The customers of your Help Desk need to know what services are available and how to request them. These services include computer system repair, application support, and access request management to controlled resources. Even though Help Desk services are usually considered an expense, many successful Help Desk managers will market their services. Customers that are aware of what services are available are more likely to have higher satisfaction with the technology they use for their job function. When the customer's technology devices are functioning well, the customer is more productive, which is a benefit to the company's financial health.

Marketing Help Desk services to internal customers are like public marketing campaigns. So how should a Help Desk manager get started in marketing the Help Desk?

How to start marketing the Help Desk

Help Desk general information – It is important to gather and document general information about your Help Desk. General information is the foundational information about your Help Desk you want everyone to know. This information includes contact information, such as the phone number and email address used to initiate customer support. It can be frustrating if a customer has an issue and they struggle to find the contact information to engage the Help Desk. If it takes more than a few minutes, they could be ticked off, making the support interaction more difficult. Therefore, this information should be included in welcome guides, quick reference guides, and website resources. Additional general information to include in your marketing efforts is the hours of operation, URLs of the support portal, and such.

Welcome Guide – First impressions are long-lasting. It is important to provide new company employees with a welcome guide, which will outline company services available. A welcome guide should include the Help Desk's general information. This general information should include hours of operation and contact channels. It should include the getting started information needed for a new user using company technology such as email, voicemail, and company-wide applications. Providing proactive solution steps in the welcome guide for the most commonly asked Help Desk questions will reduce the overall call volume from new users. Many companies which offer a welcome guide will partner with HR, Facilities, and other departments to include helpful new hire information.

Quick Reference Guides – These are instructions that are condensed to a page or two providing users information as they need it. Providing quick reference cards in a welcome guide, online, or as a handout will greatly improve user productivity and reduce calls to the Help Desk. Reducing Help Desk calls reduce Help Desk expenses. Content for quick reference cards usually focuses on high Help Desk call volume issues, which the customers could solve with the correct instruction. A few examples of quick reference card topics could be how to perform self-service password resets, setting up a default printer, configuring email on your mobile device, and voicemail setup instructions. Quick reference guides are also very helpful when rolling out a new application or service.

Help Desk website/portal – A Help Desk online customer portal helps customers to be informed and productive. A typical Help Desk portal lets customers request help via a support ticket, check the status of a current support ticket, or search through previous tickets. This self-service type functionality is expected by customers, and it's huge cost savings for the Help Desk. Most Help Desk ticketing applications will have ways to place an interface directly on the website and portal to make customer interaction very transparent.

Informational Roadshows – As a Help Desk manager, it is important to network with department leadership and staff in their environment. Try scheduling events with departments and put on a presentation demonstrating what IT services the Help Desk offers. This could include handing out quick reference guides, running a PowerPoint overview slideshow, and hosting a real-time projector walkthrough of your support web portal. This is also a great time to introduce members of your Help Desk staff. Customers will appreciate seeing the smiling faces of the Help Desk staff, which have been providing phone support over the years. Most importantly, reserve able time for questions and answers.

Brown Bag Sessions – A brown bag session is a topic-focused meeting that occurs during a lunch period. Since participants or the meeting host provide lunch during the session, it has been commonly referred to as a brown bag meeting. This meeting format is a great way for the Help Desk to deliver specific information to their customers while promoting the Help Desk's service offerings.

Technology Fairs – A technology fair is usually greater than just the Help Desk. A technology fair is usually hosted by the entire Information Technology department. It is an opportunity for the Information Technology department to display the systems used, the service available, and the staff. Having the Help Desk at the technology fair is a great way to market the Help Desk services.

Marketing the Help Desk Worksheet

Below are several projects to start marketing the Help Desk. For each of these projects, you should have a person assigned to lead the effort.

Step 1 - General Information

Gathering, organizing, and providing general Help Desk information is the first step in marketing your services.

1. Gather all the official Help Desk general information.
   a. Phone number
   b. Email address
   c. Website or portal URL
   d. Social Media
   e. Hours of operation
   f. If applicable, after-hours information
2. Ensure all contact mediums are working correctly and you have the most up-to-date addresses.
3. Create a standard general information template to be used in all Help Desk publications, distributed material, and online presence.
4. Notify the entire staff that including the general information template in any customer-facing material is mandatory.

Step 2 - Welcome Guide

A new employee welcome guide featuring Help Desk services available is one of the most important marketing tools you can implement.

1. Create or update an existing welcome guide. Include the following information in the welcome guide.

a. Include the general information gathered in step 1.
   b. Include getting started type information needed for a new employee using company technology such as email, voicemail, and login information.
   c. Include quick reference guides for commonly used applications.
   d. Frequently asked questions and solutions should also be included, such as how to reset passwords with the self-service tool.
   e. Important new employee information from other departments such as facilities and HR should also be included.
2. Create a process to place the welcome guide where the new employee will receive it on their first day of work. Typically, it is placed along with their newly assigned computer. If they are working remotely, send the welcome guide with the laptop shipped.
3. Every month run a report on all Help Desk tickets created for last month's new employees. This will help you identify what questions they asked and the issues they reported. Analyzing this information may lead to welcome guide updates.
4. Meet with new employees to obtain feedback about the welcome guide and onboarding process.

Step 3 - Informational Roadshows

1. Meet with department leaders and request an opportunity to give a Help Desk presentation during their team meeting or another event.
2. Run a report on the Help Desk tickets recently created for the department users.
3. Create a presentation to show the department users what their most frequent issues and questions are. Provide tips and solutions to these issues and questions.

4. Have an open question period on the agenda so a Help Desk representative can answer questions the audience may have.
5. Document the meeting discussion and ensure to act on any follow-up items from the meeting.

Step 4 - Technology Fairs

1. Seek approval from HR and IT leadership to hold a technology fair on the company property.
2. Meet with Information Technology managers to enlist their team's participation in the technology fair. Each manager should host a booth or table to display their area of expertise.
3. Secure a location to hold the technology fair. Suggested areas are conference rooms, large hallway, courtyard, or other outdoor areas.

Chapter 22

Typical Customer Issues

> **Chapter Objectives**
> - Learn the top 10 customer issues reported to the Help Desk.
> - Understand some of the common solutions to those issues.
> - Review the overall recommendations.

Customers are the lifeblood of the company. Understanding why your customers call the Help Desk is critical. Analyzing the most frequently occurring questions and issues will help you improve the customer experience. A happy customer is a repeat customer and will provide word a mouth advertising. This also applies to customers who are fellow internal employees. If internal or external customers are treated poorly, there are always negative consequences.

User Issue #1 - I can't remember my password

This is the most asked question of any Help Desk. Help Desks see a high volume of password calls in the mornings, after a weekend, after a holiday, and after a change to their old password. One-way companies are enforcing security is by requiring their employees to use complex passwords. Complex passwords are passwords that are greater than eight characters, include numbers and special characters, and have not been used as a password recently. Complex passwords are a good security measure, but this complexity can also cause problems for users. Users unable to remember a complex password can lead to higher call volume. As a Help Desk manager, what can you do?

Staffing levels – You should map out your calling volume patterns and staff appropriate during the high-volume periods such as Mondays and mornings. To staff up during these high-volume morning periods and avoid overstaffing during lower afternoon periods, you must be creative. Many employees may be open to flexible shift hours such as four ten-hour days and weekend shifts. Staffing can also be supplemented by employing part-time workers, contractors, and overflow staff from other groups.

Skill-based call routing - By using an Interactive voice response (IVR) system, users can identify they need password assistance by keypad or voice. Help Desk agents can be assigned to skill-based groups. Password assistance is generally the simplest type of support issue. So you can assign lower-skilled and less costly Help Desk agents to the password support skill group to handle the password support call. This will reduce costs per call and keep your highly skilled agents available for more complex issues.

Self-service password reset solution – This is a system that allows a user to reset their password from a web browser without calling the Help Desk. This will reduce the volume of calls to the Help Desk and reduce overall long-term costs. This also improves the productivity of a user by averting unnecessary and prolonged wait time for a Help Desk agent during high call volume periods.

User issue #2 - My computer is so slow

A slow computer is a symptom of a larger issue. While there are many solutions to this problem, the Help Desk agent should be coached on how to handle this in a logical problem-solving manner. Establish a timeline of when it started to slow down. Was it this morning or last week? Establishing a timeline can help you troubleshoot. For example, if the issue just started today, you can look at a potential virus, a new application installed, a recently applied security patch, or a change in user behavior. If it has been occurring for a longer period and getting worse, it could be more hardware or system related.

User issue #3 - I can't print anything

Printer issues can be challenging since there are five variables that could be the culprit. These five variables are the printer, the computer, the application, the print server, or the network. It is important to create a knowledge article to assist the Help Desk agent in troubleshooting. I like to start troubleshooting from the printer and work back to the application.

- Is the printer powered up online and not displaying any errors such as a paper jam?
- Is it a locally attached printer, and are the cables connected?
- Is it a network printer, and can anyone else print to it?
- Is the printer installed on the computer, is it the default printer, and what is the status?
- When did it last print?
- Have you ever printed with this application, and is the correct printer selected?

User issue #4 - I can't get my mobile device to sync my emails

This is a frequent problem for mobile device users that can be frustrating. Configuration and syncing problems can result in the mail not being updated, calendar meetings not being up to date, and problems with your contacts.

- Ensuring the mail account settings on the mail server are critical to ensuring the user can sync. Ensure your staff has the knowledge and access for this.
- Ensuring the customer is using the correct application and have the correct local setting is also important.
- Did the user recently change passwords? Sometimes a recent domain password change can cause a sync issue.
- Many companies will provide a walk-up service or deskside support to reduce the time it takes to resolve sync issues.

User issue #5 - The Internet/network is slow

Users understand when things are not working the same as the day before. If the network or Internet seems slow, they will contact the Help Desk. When the Help Desk is answering these calls, they should have up-to-date information if there are any network or Internet web content filter issues. If there are, Help Desk management should post a front-end message on the Help Desk phone system to alert users as they call. Also, the Help Desk agents should receive an outage or issue notice so that they can save time troubleshooting.

User issue #6 - My application is not working or is slow

Application support can be the most challenging type of call since most Help Desks have hundreds of applications they support. The best way to ensure your Help Desk agents can solve a high percentage of application support calls is to have a good knowledge base full of solutions. The solutions should be searchable by application name and error codes. Many successful knowledge base solutions will have the main landing page for each major application and then have links to specific issues/solutions from that landing page. Analyzing the resolution data from previous application issues escalations can also be helpful. These are tickets escalated to and solved by application engineers and developers. These solutions should be reviewed by the application engineers and developers and then incorporated into the knowledge base.

User issue #7 - I have deleted some files; can I get them back?

Users can have many issues related to lost or deleted files. Some users will inappropriately store documents and data on their local computers. It is important that users receive training and guidance on proper ways of saving files to the network before they have a problem. Companies will back up and be able to recover files stored on a network drive. If the user is missing files from a local drive, recovery may not be an option.

User issue #8 - How do I connect my mobile device to the guest network?

With most employees and visitors having their own mobile devices, your company needs a policy for guest wireless access. Most companies offer guests wireless access and allow what is called Bring Your Own Device (BYOD). The guest network allows users to reach the Internet without allowing access to the internal network and company resources. In most cases, access is secured by a password and certificate to control access. To make this work, the users may have to select a network and add in their login information. This typically generates several calls to the Help Desk. To avoid generating calls, we recommend posting the steps to configure access to the guest network. Places to post this information include the front desk, training rooms, conference rooms, and break rooms.

User issue #9 - The website I need is blocked

Many companies use web content filters to limit users from accessing potentially harmful websites. Companies may also block social media, video sharing, and questionable content websites. However, there are always exceptions to rules for business needs. Make sure your Help Desk has a way to submit a customer request to unblock a website. This typically can be done by the website address or by user account. If the Help Desk does not have the authority to unblock a website, make sure they know how long the review SLA is. Customers will want to know a timeframe for the review to occur.

User issue #10 - How do I reset my voicemail password?

The important thing to remember for supporting voicemail issues is to provide your Help Desk agents with a good troubleshooting script. The script can include popular error codes and symptoms of voicemail issues. Proper training for voicemail issues should be offered by the Telecom team. It is also important to document the actions taken into a ticket for future calls or if deskside support is needed.

Chapter 23

Customer service complaints

> **Chapter Objectives**
> - Learn the top customer service complaints.
> - Understand some of the common solutions to those complaints.
> - Review the overall recommendations.

If you have managed or worked at a Help Desk for any amount of time, you may have heard of many customer service complaints occurring repeatedly. Many of these issues are not unique, and they transcend all industries. The good news is throughout this book; together, we identify the issues and the solutions to fix them. The leading causes of customer service complaints are actually well known, but for some reason, the Help Desk and call center still struggle. Below are a few of the major area that causes customer service complaints.

The incident was not resolved on the first contact (FCR)

Users can put up with many customer service issues if the problem is resolved. However, when a user contacts the Help Desk and their issue is not resolved, they feel upset. Being able to resolve the incident on the first contact is a foundational measurement of the maturity of the

Help Desk. Industry-standard FCR, when including password unlocks and resets, is about 80% successful. When you have an incident, which cannot be solved, it is important to show empathy and apologize for not solving this issue immediately. You want to reassure the customer that you will escalate this issue. Most importantly, you should provide an estimated time when it will be fixed or when you will provide an update. So what are some ways to improve FCR?

Actively listen - Listen to the customer to describe their issue. Don't assume you know the issue before the customer is done explaining. Many Help Desk agents will rush to a solution only later to fix they do not completely understand the issue being described.

Use your knowledge base - Provide Help Desk agents with a knowledge base that is searchable and efficient to provide solutions to the issues.

Check the history - Check previously reported issues by the customers for clues of recent sessions of support.

Current Trends - Check the Help Desk team's recently opened tickets to see if a similar issue has been reported or if there is a company-wide outage. Many times, unusual issues with applications and websites impact all users verse a single user.

Customer callback

It's bad enough if you cannot resolve the incident on the first contact, but it is worse if you have to call the customer back for more information. Customers think once they hang up after the first call that you are working to resolve their issue. If you call back and ask initial questions, they will know no progress has been made. So how do you avoid excessive customer callbacks?

Capture all the information – It is important to capture all of the required information during the first contact. This means validating the contact information of the customer. It also means documenting all the symptoms shared by the customer and all of the support steps performed into the Help Desk ticket.

Keep promises - If you convey when the issue will be resolved or when a status update will be provided, make sure you meet it.

Ensure resolution – Sometimes, when a ticket has been escalated to a second-level team, they are able to resolve the issue. It is important to remember the customer must agree that the issue has been resolved. To receive customer confirmation that the issue has been resolved, it is best to contact the customer directly to ensure all is working well.

Long resolution time

Have you ever worked at a Help Desk, and their list of open tickets is weeks or months old? Can you imagine how frustrating it would be if you were the customer and your issue was not addressed?

Service Level Management - Many companies implement service level management with SLAs that customers and the Help Desk agree to a set expectation of how long something will take to be resolved. If a ticket comes close to breaching the SLA and is not resolved yet, a warning will alert the Help Desk agent so they can update the customer.

Phone Tree Greeting

Have you ever called a customer service phone number and had an endless menu of prompts? Press 1 for this, press 2 for that, and so on. While using a phone tree is a useful tool, it can also cause customer dissatisfaction if overused. So what are some of the phone tree complaints by customers?

Endless menu selections – Using phone tree menu selections is a great way to perform skill-based routing, which will route the caller to an agent group most familiar with the customer's menu selection. Also, you can use phone tree menu selections for static information recordings such as the company's address and hours of operation. What customers do not like is more than four choices on the front menu and then following levels with even more choices. When developing a phone tree diagram, each selection should have a strong argument on why it is needed. For example, adding a selection for password help can route a customer to an entry-level Help Desk agent to handle the easy password unlock and allow Help Desk agents with higher skills to take the more advanced issues.

Dead ends – How frustrating is it when a customer selects menu after menu and then ends up in an incorrect spot, with no main menu option? Sometimes, phone trees will play a short recorded statement and then disconnect you.

No exit ramp – Phone trees can help companies reduce costs, route callers to the correct support resource, and overall make the process more efficient. However, many people want to speak to a human ultimately. In every call tree, there should be an option to exit the call tree and be put in contact with the next available support person.

Customer Service Etiquette

One important factor in improving customer satisfaction and reducing customer service complaints is promoting positive customer service etiquette. It is very important that you Help Desk agents have positive interactions, which will lead to positive results.

Language – A customer will call the helpdesk for help because they don't understand the technical issue and how to fix it. The last thing they want to hear from the Help Desk agent is technical jargon. Speak the common language and express technical steps in a way that anyone can understand.

Show empathy – Technical issues can annoy or even anger a customer. It can be hard to work with or satisfy an angry customer unless you show some empathy. It is common practice for the Help Desk agent to diffuse the anger by acknowledging the anger and showing empathy. Once the customer knows you care and their frustration is acknowledged, you can work as a partner in resolving the issue.

Be positive and polite – Nothing improves customer satisfaction like a positive interaction between the Help Desk agent and the customer. Help Desk agents that are polite, smile through the phone, and use positive words will always score high in their customer satisfaction surveys.

Overall recommendations to reduce customer service complaints

- Use the language of your customers.
- Be positive and polite.
- Respond promptly to requests.
- Be transparent include the customer in the process.
- Capture all details in the support ticket.
- Review the customer's previous support tickets.
- Empathize and follow up on customer complaints.
- Owning the customer's issue until resolved.

Chapter 24

Total Contact Ownership

If a customer contacts a Help Desk with an issue and the Help Desk is unable to resolve its first contact, it can be disappointing. We do understand not every issue can be solved on the first contact by the Help Desk, but too many times and escalated requests for help seem to go into a black hole. If tickets pile up with escalation groups, no updates are provided to the customer and lingering customer IT issues occur, it may impact overall company productivity. One method to build a culture of accountability to the customer is to implement Total Contact Ownership.

The principle of Total Contact Ownership is whoever takes the first customer issue will own the issue until it has been resolved. Some refer to this as owning the issue from the cradle to the grave. This means if the issue cannot be resolved on the first contact, the Help Desk agent will follow the ticket through the escalation path. They will provide timely updates to the customer and ensure that the ticket does not linger in a non-resolved status. Both the Help Desk agent and escalation groups work to resolve the issue while the service level agreement clock is ticking. Customer-focused Help Desks using Total Contact Ownership will ensure customer issues are addressed and resolved in a timely manner.

The benefits of implementing Total Contact Ownership.

First Contact Resolution (FCR)

Help Desk management will see a significant increase in resolving issues on the first contact. In a low-performing Help Desk, an agent will try and help a customer resolve their issue. If they are unsuccessful, they will reassign the ticket to the escalation group and move on to the next caller. Basically, the agent is washing their hands of this issue, at least for the time being. With TCO, Help Desk agents know they own the ticket, and they have a vested interest to ensure it is resolved correctly. Resolving the customer's issue without escalating it to another group improves their FCR and overall performance statistics.

If the agent must escalate the issue ticket, they will want to understand how the escalation group ultimately resolves the issue. They will follow the ticket and read the IT Engineer's notes. If a knowledge article is needed, the Help Desk agent may lead an effort to create one. This will provide a solution article if another caller calls with the same type of issue. This means the actions and article just improved the first contact resolution rate at your Help Desk.

Employee Engagement

The Help Desk agent engagement will improve with the agent having a sense of ownership and empowerment of the ticket and process. Most Help Desk agents thrive on achievement. If a customer issue is solved, the result most likely will be a happy customer. Agents really feed off this positive interaction. The agent will feel a sense of accomplishment and pride. Pride in the ownership of a successfully resolved support ticket. Ultimately employee engagement will improve both individually and for the Help Desk team as a whole.

Performance management

After implementing total contact ownership, the quality of the work per Help Desk agent will also improve. With TCO, there are a lot of process steps for the agent to follow. Some of these steps include good ticket documentation, a structured status update provided to the customer, and proper management of active tickets. Eventually, the Help Desk agent will be accustomed to the TCO process, and the good habits will become baked in. Help Desk supervisors will see that their staff will reduce aging ticket load, reduce sloppy ticket documentation issues, and should see a significant improvement in First Contact Resolution. The performance of the Help Desk agent in resolving and closing tickets must be measured both in volume and duration. This will lead to identifying coaching opportunities, knowledge article improvements, and process improvements.

Customer Satisfaction

Nothing is better for a customer is to have their issue resolved quickly on their first contact with the Help Desk. If an issue must be escalated to a group outside the Help Desk, customers like to be kept in the loop of their request for help. Sometimes resolutions may take a while. With TCO, frequent and regular customer updates are essential. Sharing updates will go a long way in improving the customer experience and, ultimately, customer satisfaction.

Customers that call a Help Desk that has implemented Total Contact Ownership feel they have a voice. The customer feels that someone is looking out for them. They feel confident that when they report an issue, the issue will be addressed properly and in a timely manner.

Total Contact Ownership procedure best practices

Creating a procedure for the total contact ownership process is important. The Help Desk agents needed to know what was required of them. A mature Help Desk can incorporate additional steps in the incident management and service request management procedures. These steps are important to document to ensure the Help Desk agent is maintaining ownership of their tickets. Make sure the following total contact ownership best practices are part of the procedure.

- If the Help Desk agent is unable to resolve the issue, they should attempt to warm transfer the issue to the escalation group. If the escalation group is unavailable, then the Help Desk agent will monitor the ticket to ensure that it becomes assigned to an engineer.
- The Help Desk agent will provide a regular update on the status of the ticket to the customer.
- If the Help Desk Agent is the owner of too many tickets, the agent should be given opportunities off the phone to catch up on ticket status and documentation.
- When an engineer from the escalation resolves the issue, the Help Desk agent will review the ticket's support notes. If there is not enough information or the Help Desk agent does not understand the support notes, the Help Desk agent will contact the engineer.
- Before closing the ticket and issue, the Help Desk agent will obtain approval from the customer that the issue has been resolved.
- After resolving and closing the ticket, the Help Desk agent will ensure that a knowledge article has been created to capture the resolution steps for a future incident.

Placing customers first with Total Contact Ownership

To significantly improve customer satisfaction at your Help Desk, implementing Total Contact Ownership is a great step. The Help Desk will become accountable to the customers they support and lead to more engaged employees.

Total Contact Ownership worksheet

The keys to successfully implementing Total Contact Ownership are common sense and straightforward.

Step 1 – Create and document the total contact ownership process.

Ensure you incorporate the total contact ownership best practices outlined in this chapter are reflected in your incident management, service request management, customer handling, and ticket handling procedures.

Step 2 – Train the staff on the total contact ownership process.

Once the total contact ownership process has been created and documented, then the Help Desk agents need to be trained. Help Desk agent training on the new process is critical to the overall success. The Help Desk agents and the escalation groups must receive proper training and set expectations for the process. Use the training and development best practices identified in the corresponding chapter. Remember the total contact ownership best practices cover many areas. These areas include the following.

- ticket escalation
- customer updates
- overall agent ticket workload
- engineer support notes
- customer approvals for closure

- creating knowledge articles for new resolution steps.

Step 3 – Communicate with the customer about the total contact ownership process.

Communicating the new total contact ownership process to customers is also critical to the overall success. The customers should be provided an overview of the process. They also should understand that there will be an owner of their issue identified and tracking the issue to closure.

Step 4 – Provide reporting on the total contact ownership status.

There are a lot of different reports that can be generated related to total contact ownership. Some of the important reports are the following.
- Total open tickets
- Tickets opened by the customer
- Tickets opened by Help Desk agent owner
- First Contact Resolution rates. The FCR rates should be improving as total contact ownership matures.

Step 5 – Meet with the customer on the total contact ownership SLAs.

The customer is kept up to date with the entire resolution process and status updates from the Help Desk agent who owns the ticket. Many departments and customer groups may have Service Level Agreements (SLA)s setup with the Help Desk. These Service Level Agreements with the Help Desk and escalation group have a pre-negotiated timeframe to resolve the incident reported by the customer. During the meetings, some of the total contact ownership reports created in the previous step may be helpful to share.

IT Service Management

The Help Desk has many ties to IT service management. IT Service Management, using the ITIL framework, governs how IT services are delivered to customers. By developing policies and supporting procedures, IT Service Management delivers repeatable, efficient, and continuously improving service to meet customers' needs.

In the following chapters, we will be focusing mainly on ITIL Service Operation processes. Service operation covers executing service delivery, operations, and support. While not every process is solely in the Help Desk realm, the Help Desk does have many inputs and outputs to these processes. Specifically, we will be discussing incident management. We will review how to create an incident management procedure and then discuss the major incident management process. We will then discuss problem management and the linkages between incident management and the Help Desk. Since most of the incidents the Help Desk handles are caused by a change, we will be reviewing the change management process.

Chapter 25

Incident Management Best Practices

Chapter Objectives

- Understand what an incident is.
- Identify the benefits of an incident management program.
- Outline the components of an incident management procedure.
- Review incident prioritization.
- How to implement an incident management communication plan.

The Help Desk is great at responding to a customer if they are seeking something new with a request for service. In addition, the Help Desk is very adept at handling the process of fixing things when broken. When customers have technology items that are broken, the Help Desk is engaged with the incident management process. To be a mature Help Desk responsive to your customers, your company will have an incident management program implemented. While an incident management program will include more groups than just the Help Desk, the Help Desk plays a major role. As a single point of contact, the Help Desk will be the first and last contact for your customers having issues. A Help Desk is the first point of contact by receiving calls from customers, event alerts from monitoring, and engagements from social media channels. The Help Desk is the last point of contact by communicating and confirming the incident resolution with the customer before closing the incident.

Having a program to manage incidents will make your Help Desk team responsive to your customer's issues and improve customer satisfaction. It will ensure a repeatable response to issues and meet customer expectations. This repeatable response will ensure proper incident escalation to resolver groups. Communication procedures will ensure the customer is informed. Incident tickets will have a consistent format and will be used as an official historical record. A mature incident management process is a core function of the Help Desk.

What is an Incident?

An incident is an unplanned interruption or quality reduction to an IT service. The goal of having an established incident management process is to return the service to normal functionality quickly while minimizing the impact on the business. Normal functioning operations of an IT service are defined in Service Level Agreements (SLA) or other agreements between the business and IT operations.

In a real-world example, an incident is not a user request for access to or the installation of a financial application. An incident is when a user had access to an installed financial application, and now it is not working or has a fault. Also, the fault is not planned by a scheduled maintenance outage but is unplanned and not intended.

Benefits of an Incident Management Program

There are many benefits for a company to have an incident management program. Companies with an incident management program see the availability of IT services and customer satisfaction survey scores improve. We have documented some of the more well-known benefits.

Higher IT service availability

A mature incident management procedure will lead to higher IT service availability by prioritizing critical incidents and focusing limited resources on resolving them first. Having an incident management program will standardize incident handling processes. With a standard process in place, established criteria will lead to better prioritization of incidents based on impact and urgency. Once the highest priority incidents are identified, incident resolving resources can focus their attention on these IT service-impacting incidents to resolve them quickly. This reduction of time to resolve high-priority incidents will improve IT service availability.

Often, a significant amount of low and medium-priority incidents in a short period of time may be a precursor to a larger IT service outage. Incident management can help identify if a relationship exists between these incidents and create a higher priority parent incident. Identifying incident trends, relating them together, and focusing attention on resolving these incidents can reduce the chance of a full-blown IT service outage. Avoiding an IT service outage will mean that the service can remain available even though it may have been partially degraded for a period of time.

Increased customer satisfaction

An incident management procedure will ensure customer issues are handled with a consistent process. Over time the process can be analyzed and improved to be more successful in resolving incidents quicker. Customers will appreciate a repeatable experience since they will know what to expect when they call the Help Desk. They really will appreciate having their issue solved faster. The result of this repeatable incident handling experience may lead to a positive improvement in customer satisfaction survey feedback.

Enterprise reporting improvements

By creating and updating an incident ticket with the support interactions, customers will benefit from the ticket status transparency. A historical documented record will be available for future reporting, data mining, and troubleshooting issues. Following the mature procedures of an incident management program will lead to better reporting on all IT services. Companies with an incident management program realize that enterprise reporting will be much improved. Reporting options such as real-time ticket trends as well as monthly system performance reports will be invaluable for many stakeholders.

Fundamentals of an Incident Management Program

For an incident management program to be successful, you must make sure your team is creating an incident ticket, assigning incident priority, escalating the incident as needed to appropriate resolver groups, and following up with the customer before closing the Help Desk Incident ticket. As a new Help Desk manager, you must audit the incident management process to ensure incident priority is set correctly, ticket classification categories are functional, and escalated ticket queues are being managed appropriately.

While each company's incident management procedures are similar, there are unique factors to be considered to understand how to create an incident management procedure. We have created this incident management procedure best practices step-by-step guide to help you build a procedure that works for your team and company.

Incident Management Procedure Fundamentals

Creating an incident management procedure may seem straightforward. However, there are some key components you need not to overlook when developing your incident management procedure. By including guidance on change history, the scope, and setting foundational principles, your process implementation will have a greater chance of succeeding.

Components of an incident management procedure

Incident Management Change History

Once implemented, issues may arise with your incident management process. These issues may require you to make a change. Changes to your incident management process should not be taken lightly. Failure to follow a formal change process will lead to a breakdown of the process. Stakeholders, customers, and staff will need to know of significant changes proposed, have input on the changes, and receive notice that a change is occurring to the incident management procedure. Once you have obtained approval to update the incident management procedure, the change history section should identify a change that has been made. The change history should document the new procedure version number, change author, description of the change, and the date of the change. Always keep previous versions of the procedure in an archived location.

Table of Contents

Adding a table of contents to your incident management procedure will make it easy for your reader to find a section quickly. During a critical incident, having a table of contents could save valuable time for your staff.

The purpose statement of incident management

Stating the purpose of the incident management procedure is important for the reader. This section can be short, but it must be clear. An example of a purpose is "The purpose of the Incident management process is to handle and resolve all incidents involving IT personnel in a consistent, timely, professional, and cost-effective manner."

The objective of your incident management procedure

The objectives of the incident management process will support the purpose. The objectives can also be used to focus on the incident management team on why we have an incident management process. The objectives can be used to benchmark the effectiveness and maturity of the process. We have created a list of the most common objectives that may be included in the incident management procedure.

> **Incident management procedure objectives**
>
> - To resolve an incident as quickly and efficiently as possible.
> - To ensure client satisfaction with the quality of support.
> - To provide a consistent and repeatable process for incidents.
> - Ensure the process is beneficial for the Information Technology department while minimizing the bureaucratic impact on the customer and support communities
> - Supply accurate and timely information pertaining to incidents.
> - To use common process and tools for providing customer support that provides:
>   - Usability and responsiveness to enable quick call entry.
>   - Measurements to understand the workload.
>   - Continuous review and improvement of the current tools and processes.
> - The process establishes efficient output into other defined and approved processes as inputs.

Scope

The scope section lets the reader know what is included and excluded from coverage by this incident management procedure. If you do not define what is in and out of scope, someone else will. Don't overwhelm your new process. Clearly define what is in and out of scope. Just because something is determined to be out of scope, it does not mean there is not a process for it. It just means that there may be a separate process specifically designed for the out-of-scope item, and it is not managed by this incident management process.

In-scope

This section identifies what is in scope. Typically, this describes those incidents reported by supported customers, managed in the ticketing application, and supported by IT are in-scope. Examples of this are;

All incidents are created and managed in the [company name] ticketing application.

All incidents reported by [customer groups]

All incidents managed by the [department name]

Out of scope

Defining what is out of scope is critical. Not being specific could lead to confusion, disagreements, and overwhelming your resources. Out of scope example items are;

All service requests are out of scope.

All project-related work is out of scope.

All incidents not managed in the [company name] ticketing application should be out of scope.

Specific criteria related to excluding customers or support groups should be stated.

Business Principles

Business Principles will set your incident management best practices as foundational rules for your department. Below are some general incident management best practices.

Incident Owner – Identifying the incident ticket owner is important to ensure that all activities are occurring in a timely manner. These activities include monitoring, tracking, and communicating status updates to both customers and Help Desk staff. All communication with the customer will be documented in the incident ticket. Typically the Help Desk Agent will be identified as the Incident Owner for all incident tickets they create.

Incident Tickets - All contacts and interactions with the customer must be documented in an incident ticket. If it is not documented, then it did not happen.

Incident Priority – The incident priority or severity should be set by using an incident priority matrix. It is important to prioritize incident tickets so normal operations can be restored as quickly as possible in a prioritized fashion, with the highest priority incident receiving the most immediate attention.

New Incidents - If the customer is contacting the Help Desk about a new issue, the Help Desk Agent will create a new incident ticket and will fill out all appropriate ticket fields.

Existing Incidents – If the customer is contacting the Help Desk about an existing issue, the Help Desk Agent will search for existing tickets and will provide the user with a status update. The incident ticket must be updated with a summary of the interaction.

Escalation Queue Management – If the Help Desk is unable to resolve an incident and requires assistance, the Help Desk Agent will assign the incident ticket to the appropriate escalation queue. An escalation queue is a holding area for an escalated ticket from which the escalated work team receives their work. The Manager of the escalation queue to which the incident has been assigned will ensure the appropriate resources are monitoring the queue for newly assigned incident tickets. A member of the escalation queue will acknowledge the incident ticket and identify themselves as the assignee of the incident ticket. If the issue and customer information required to perform the resolution activities are missing, or if it was assigned to the wrong escalation group, the assignee or escalation queue manager will assign the ticket back to the Help Desk queue with a documented reason for the reassignment.

VIP Users – This section will provide guidance on how a VIP is identified. Typically a VIP user has been noted in the profile of the user in the ticketing application. This section will also identify what additional level of service VIP users will receive.

Incident resolution – The incident ticket should be resolved when the service has been restored to standard operation, which may be a permanent fix or a temporary workaround. Incidents should not be moved to a status of "resolved" until service has been restored.

Incident closure – Incidents should not be moved to a status of "closed" until the incident resolution has been confirmed with the customer. The Help Desk should have an incident closure process if the Help Desk Agent is unable to make contact with the customer after multiple attempts. We recommend that the Help Desk staff will attempt to contact the customer three (3) times by two (2) different methods (example, phone, and e-mail) in a minimum five (5) business day period before moving the incident to a "closed" status.

Incident reopens – An incident in a "closed" status should never be reopened. If the customer's previously resolved incident reoccurs again, a new incident ticket should be opened. The new incident ticket can be related to the previous incident ticket.

Root Cause Analysis (RCA) – Root cause analysis (RCA) is a method used to uncover the cause of a problem using well-established techniques and tools. In Information Technology, the RCA is used by problem management to find and eliminate the cause of incidents. At a minimum, all priority one or critical incidents should have a problem management investigation ticket opened for a root cause analysis. The incident and problem ticket should be related, and a formal findings report should be generated.

Customer Contact Channels

Your incident management procedure should identify all customer contact channels that can be used to generate an incident ticket. Customer contact channels are the methods used by the customer to request help or report a service interruption. Examples of frequently used customer contact channels include phone, email, customer portal, walk-up, and chat. System monitoring should also be included if monitoring events automatically create incident tickets. In addition to what customer contact channels may be used is to define any specific needs defined on how they should be used.

Incident Prioritization

Due to Help Desk resource constraints, not all incidents can be worked on simultaneously. The work order of incident tickets will need to be determined. This work order of incident tickets is based on the priority assigned to the incident tickets. The priority of the incident is based on the impact and urgency of the issue. The incident impact is the potential financial, brand, or security damage caused by the incident on the business organization before it can be resolved. Urgency is how quickly incident resolution is required. The incident priority is a matrix of impact and urgency. Below is an incident priority matrix example.

Priority Matrix					
		Impact			
		Critical	High	Medium	Low
Urgency	Critical	1	1	2	3
	High	1	2	3	3
	Medium	2	3	3	4
	Low	3	3	4	5

In our priority matrix example, we used critical, high, medium, and low as criteria with impact and urgency. To be effective and give guidance to staff assigning an incident priority, you need to define what the criteria mean. An example of this guidance is the following.

Impact

Critical - A core business IT service is unavailable, causing a direct financial, brand, or security impact on the business organization.

High - An IT service is unavailable or degraded, impacting a large group of users.

Medium - An incident impacting a VIP or a small group of users.

Low - A single user incident.

Urgency

Critical - A core business IT service is unavailable and must be restored immediately to minimize a direct financial, brand, or security impact on the business organization.

High - An IT service is unavailable or degraded, impacting a large group of users, and must be restored within 4 hours to minimize a direct financial, brand, or security impact on the business organization.

Medium - An incident impacting a VIP or a small group of users.

Low - A single user incident.

Incident Management Communication Plan

A proactive Help Desk team will have Incident Management Communication Plan in place to follow when an outage to a service occurs. In advance of an outage, it is important to develop a well-thought-out Incident Management Communication Plan detailing how people will be initially notified, what information they need, when status updates will be communicated, and what resolution steps occur when a service has been restored. Answer the following questions about the state of your Incident Management Communication Plan.

Do you have a defined Incident Management Communication Plan to follow when there is an outage to a major service? Have people been trained and know how to access the plan?

Are your customers and business groups proactively informed of when a service is down, or do they generate a large volume of calls to the Help Desk?

Are your Help Desk staff members immediately informed about the outage and provided support information such as available workarounds and an estimated time for recovery?

Are members of the technology leadership department immediately aware of service outages, or are they the "last to know"?

The answer to all of these questions should be yes. If you answered no to any of these questions, we would help you put an incident management communication plan in place.

Incident Management Communication

Customers of service, technical service support staff, and service owners rely on the Incident Management team to obtain the latest status of a service outage and recovery. Incident Management Communication is typically handled in a coordinated effort via email, text messages, voicemail, web portal messages, and phone bridges. Incident Management communication reduces call volume to the Help Desk, allows the business to adjust their work activities, facilitates greater collaboration to resolve the incident, and keeps the leadership team informed of the status.

Objectives of Incident Management Communication Plan

Prepared action plan - Have a detailed approved Incident Management Communication action plan documented and readily available for support staff to follow.

Defined general recipient list - Have up-to-date communication distribution groups defined and communication tools in place to send incident status messages. These include the incident start time, regular status updates, and incident resolution meaning the IT service is now available.

IT service-specific recipient list - Ensure customers of a service, the leadership team, and technical staff is informed of the start and end of unscheduled outages.

Workaround communication - Ensure that any workarounds are communicated to the proper groups that use the service.

Sharing technical information - Provide detailed recovery information related to the outage to technical groups. Anytime one IT service has an issue, other IT services can be impacted by the outage or even the implemented fix.

Output to problem management - Provide a post-incident summary to the problem management team related to the service.

Customer Focused Incident Management Communication

The goal of customer Incident Management Communication is to let the customer know a service is down and provide some basic information without a lot of technical jargon. Customers just want to know what service is down, what workarounds are in place, and when will an IT service be available again. This will allow the customer to make business decisions to maximize their resources. It may mean that they can perform internal communication, provide business direction, inform their customers, and let some of the workforce take a break or leave early if applicable.

Customer Focused Incident Management Communication template

Below are the core elements of a customer-focused incident management communication template. The goal of this template is to prepopulate as much needed message and text structure before an incident occurs. This template will allow your team to craft a professional, repeatable message during a time of high activity and stress.

Communication Template Name – Saving the template with a name that explicitly describes the template is important. This is to make sure the person drafting the message will use the correct template if you have more than one variation. Template examples include customer, business, leadership, and specific IT service templates.

Recipient list – The template should specifically identify who will receive the communication by referencing the recipient distribution list to use. Remember, each recipient should be added as BCC to avoid replies to all broadcast storms.

Subject line – The subject line should have a specific format used every time. A generic subject line should be developed and have bracketed placeholders when the specific service name, status, and other variables need to be entered.

Service name – The name of the service impact. Remember to use the name or names that the recipients will recognize. Instead of using a technical name such as Exchange server, use a common name such as an email server or corporate email service.

Incident start time – Remember to identify the time zone.

Status – Assigning a status such as available, degraded, or unavailable from a predefined list will eliminate confusion. This will assist you in avoiding the communication author using non-approved variations such as working, issues, or down.

High-level summary, impact, and workarounds – Remember the intended audience when entering this information. Do not use technical jargon and explain what is not working, who is impacted, and any workaround actions that can mitigate the impact.

Next update – By identifying the time when the next status update will be communicated, you will set the expectations of the uses and avoid many unnecessary calls.

For more information – It is a good practice to include the preferred method for users seeking more information. Some companies will have a dynamic web page or SharePoint site where up-to-date outage information is posted. This will allow you to avoid having to send another email when there is a small update. A link to more information could also be related to how to perform a workaround. Finally, including the contact information for the Help Desk is always appropriate.

Technical Incident Management Communication template

The Technical Incident Management Communication template is similar to the customer template but also provides the following;

Recovery efforts – When possible, a detailed timeline of recovery efforts should be sent to the technical teams. This is to ensure the teams are aware of changes and activities occurring which could impact the systems they support. This information can be obtained from the incident ticket, war-room bridge, and change tickets.

War room bridge information – The technical communication will typically include the war room bridge information, so resources are able to join the war room and assist as needed.

Action Steps

6 Steps to Start Building an Incident Management Communication Plan

- Identify your major services covered by the plan.
- Identify the customer and technical groups that will receive communication.
- Establish the frequency of updates.
- Determine the communication tools used to send incident status messages.
- Establish and format templates to be used for communication from each communication tool.
- Establish a bridge number and access code to be used only for war room bridges.

It's time to be proactive and take control of your Incident Management communication. Implementing an Incident Management

Communication Plan before an outage occurs will mature your team. The service you provide will improve customer satisfaction.

Chapter 26

Major Incident Management Best Practices

Chapter Objectives

- Define what a major incident is.
- Understand the major incident lifecycle.
- Review major incident lifecycle best practices.
- Discuss the post incident review process.

Designing a major incident management process is critical to protecting a company from significant financial loss, tarnishing its reputation, and impacting its customers. A fully optimized major incident process will leverage live monitoring, predictive analytics, and real-time alerting to proactively avoid service outages or significantly reduce Mean Time to Repair (MTTR) when an outage occurs. Unfortunately, most companies currently have a reactive or ad-hoc process. The major incident management process should be based on industry best practices, and the procedures should be standardized and continuously improved.

What is an Incident?

As stated before, ITIL defines an incident as an unplanned interruption to or quality reduction of an IT service. The goal of having an established incident management process is to return the service to normal functionality quickly while minimizing the impact on the business. Normal functioning operations of an IT service are defined in Service Level Agreements (SLA) or other agreements between the business and IT operations.

What is a Major Incident?

A major incident is an incident that demands a response and resource engagement level well beyond the routine incident management process. Therefore, a procedure for a major incident should be designed to coordinate the response and accelerate the recovery process to return the IT service to a normal state as quickly as possible. Typically, a major incident is assigned a critical priority based on an incident priority matrix of impact and urgency. Additionally, major incidents could have a high-priority assignment.

The incident priority levels typically have four levels.

1 - Critical
2 - High
3 - Medium
4 - Low

Major Incident Management Lifecycle

There is a lifecycle for major incidents, and we will review each of the phases. By reviewing what occurs in each phase, we will help you understand how the process works. From that point, we will discuss industry-standard best practices for each phase to help you process maturity.

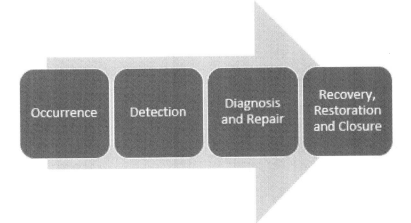

Occurrence – The occurrence phase starts when an incident to a configuration item or IT service actually starts. A high percentage of the time, the occurrence of an incident is a result of a change to a configuration item or IT service. Even though an incident has occurred for a configuration item or IT service, it has not yet been detected.

Detection - This detection phase is when event monitoring, support teams, or a user detects the issue to a configuration item or IT service. If the customer detects the issue by an error or fault, they will contact the Help Desk to report it. Other ways issues are detected through event monitoring or by the IT support teams. A mature IT support organization will identify a high percentage of issues by event monitoring and support teams versus reported by end-users.

Diagnosis and Repair – The diagnosis phase is when the initial IT support team tries to understand the incident issue. They will triage the issue and assign the priority level. If they are unable to resolve the incident at the first level, they will assign the incident to the correct escalation group to resolve the issue. The repair phase takes place once the incident is diagnosed and is the recovery action to return the configuration item to a normal state. The repair phase will continue until there is a recovery of the configuration item or IT service.

Recovery, Restoration, and Closure – In these phases, there are some subtle but important differences between recovery and restoration. Recovery is when a configuration item has returned to a normal state. The overall business service is made up of one or more configuration items that may or may not be recovered at this point. Restoration is the point when the actual business service has been recovered, and the end-users are able to use the services successfully. Closure occurs after the service is available to the user and the recovery teams validate that the service is stable from immediate reoccurrence.

Major Incident Management Lifecycle Best Practices

What specific areas are you focusing on to improve stability and availability in your environment by reducing the frequency and duration of major incidents at your company? Reducing incident Mean Time to Restore Service (MTRS) of major incidents and increasing Mean Time between Failures (MTBF) is critical. Reducing MTRS will decrease the service disruption duration to avoid a loss of sale revenue and productivity. Increasing MTBF will improve the uptime availability of your services. There are some key best practices for each of the phases of the major incident lifecycle. Understanding each phase is important to improve the capability of the IT infrastructure and IT Services.

Major Incident Lifecycle – Occurrence

The occurrence phase is when an issue to a configuration item or IT service starts until the time it has been detected. To reduce the frequency of major incidents occurring, you must study how to keep a fully functioning IT service from failing. A high percentage of the time, failure is related to a change to the configuration item or IT service. Introducing additional rigor to the change management process for higher risk changes will reduce the major incident occurrence. This extra rigor to the change management process includes better planning of the change, additional change review, and though acceptance testing after the change has been implemented

Major Incident Lifecycle – Occurrence Recommendations

Change management risk assessment calculator – When a change request is being entered, it is important to assess the risk of the change to IT services accurately and ultimately to the business. A risk calculator will prompt the change requestor to submit the change with a series of questions. The change request risk will be calculated based on the answers provided. To ensure the appropriate risk is assigned to the change, it is important to review the questions in the change risk assessment calculator. Making any needed improvements to the risk questions will more accurately identify changes that are a very high or high risk of failing. Additional scrutiny of high-risk changes may reduce the risk of causing a service interrupting incident. The risk assessment calculator is not intended to replace "human" scrutiny but will help change coordinators focus greater attention on changes that pose the greatest risks.

> **Action Steps**
>
> 1. Export all changes for the last 12 months into a spreadsheet.
> 2. Identify a target group of all failed changes, changes that caused an IT service outage, and changes that caused incidents.
> 3. Next, refine the target group to only include changes not assessed as high risk or greater.
> 4. Review the assessment questions against the change details of the target group.
> 5. Identify question updates or additions needed to assess risk more accurately.
> 6. Create an improvement project to propose and implement risk question updates.

High-Risk change implementation plans – Adjusting the risk calculator to more accurately identify high risks change is only one factor of the improvement effort. Improving the change management review process of high-risk handling changes is also an important factor. By ensuring your change implementation plans are following industry best practices, your successful change percentage should improve. There are several areas where improvements can be made.

One area of change management improvement is to determine if specific IT services have a higher frequency of failed changes. If an IT service has a history of failed changes, determine if future similar changes should be assessed with a higher risk. As an example, if changes to the accounting system experience a higher level of failed changes, any future changes to the accounting system should automatically be assigned a higher risk level.

Another area of improvement is to focus on post-change testing and validation activities. Failure to properly test the IT service during the change window may lead to an IT service outage during business hours when the IT service is being heavily used. Since the change window has been closed, an emergency change may be needed to resolve the incident outage.

System monitoring is normally set up to watch the health and performance of IT services and systems. Normally when a change is being implemented, system monitoring is placed in maintenance mode temporarily. When in maintenance mode, no alerts, errors, or incidents will be generated during the change activity in progress. When the change activity has been completed and validated, the system monitoring must be reenabled to monitor the health of the system. With system monitoring enabled, the monitoring could also find issues missed by the change validation team before the start of business. A frequent issue is that system monitoring maintenance mode duration is programmed to start and stop with a window of time that is way too excessive. This means that system monitoring could be disabled for hours after the change completion. During that time, system health is not being properly monitored. A step in the post-change validation rules should be to resume the system monitoring.

> **Action Steps**
>
> - If a change fails and causes significant incidents, add the configuration item or IT service to a fragile list requiring more scrutiny.
> - Review the change team's responsibilities and authority to ensure they are appropriate.
> - Ensure the post change testing & validation rules are comprehensive enough to identify issues during the change window.
> - Ensure post change event monitoring resumption occurs immediately after testing and validation.

Forward Schedule of Change Dashboard – If your change ticketing application supports it, build a dynamic high-risk change dashboard. The dashboard will display the real-time status of pending, in-progress, breeched, and completed high-risk changes for the current date. Everyone should be aware of the status of high-risk changes, including the data center operations staff. If IT staff are aware of a change in progress and an issue is reported to the Help Desk, there can be an immediate correlation.

Major Incident Lifecycle – Detection

Detection is when event monitoring, IT support teams, or a user detects an issue occurring to a configuration item or IT service. Once an issue is detected, an incident is logged. A mature IT support organization will identify a high percentage of incidents by event monitoring. A mature IT support organization will also detect incidents by application support teams. Less mature companies will rely on the end-users to report the issue. Early detection of issues that occurred will significantly reduce the duration of a major incident.

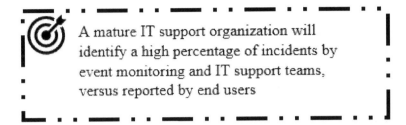

> A mature IT support organization will identify a high percentage of incidents by event monitoring and IT support teams, versus reported by end users

Major Incident Lifecycle – Detection Recommendations

Improve Service Desk Incident trending – Major incidents have a high impact on your customers. It is very important to identify support ticket trends quickly. If a trend of an unusually large number of lower priority incidents is discovered, they should be grouped into a higher priority incident based on the increased impact. Now that you have a higher priority incident, resources can be focused on the incident. To trend incidents properly, you need a well-thought-out help desk incident category scheme.

Event Monitoring – Basic monitoring is comprised of watching for spikes in system resources such as CPU utilization, memory use, and network response. Resources can investigate resource levels that rise above predetermined thresholds for an extended duration. As your event monitoring becomes more advanced, your monitoring should focus on errors with business and system transactions. By discovering errors with these transactions, issues can be corrected before they significantly affect your users. As events occur, your monitoring system will generate incident tickets for the impacted CIs based on data drive rules.

Defining CMDB CI relationships – IT services are made up of multiple configuration items. It is important to associate configuration items with IT services. Similarly, IT services should be associated with the support teams to the incident should be assigned. When a configuration item has a fault, you know what IT service is impacted. This will allow the proper resolver team to be engaged with the incident.

Incident alert and contact management – Notifying business users and support teams about the status of a major incident impacting an IT service is critical. It is important to ensure your incident alerts reach their intended targets in a timely manner. To reduce incident Mean Time to Restore Service, you must invest in an automated contact and alert management system. Many ticket applications offer this as a module. You will be able to define automated escalation rules, manage their on-call and time away scheduling, and automatically process self-managed alert subscriptions to drive a reduction in the meantime to respond.

Major Incident Lifecycle – Diagnosis and Repair

Diagnosis is when the initial IT Support team is trying to triage the configuration item fault. The first-level support team will attempt to fix the issue. If the support team is not able to fix the incident, they categorize the incident, validate the priority and escalate the incident to the correct resources to resolve. Repair is the action to return the configuration item to a normal state. Since IT services are made up of one or more configuration items, repairing a configuration item may not completely resolve the IT service incident.

Major Incident Lifecycle – Diagnosis and Repair recommendations

Incident category scheme – Proper ticket classification of an issue when a Help Desk ticket is created enables the Help Desk agent to sort the issue into support buckets. These buckets will allow knowledge to be presented to the Help Desk agent when trying to provide proper support, enable proper routing of escalated tickets, and allow trend reporting of ticket types. Ticket categories also can be used to identify mission-critical services. If an incident is raised against a mission-critical service, the priority can be elevated.

Incident priority levels – Due to IT support resource constraints, not all incidents can be worked on simultaneously. Incident tickets will need to be prioritized based on impact and urgency. The incident impact is the potential financial, brand, or security damage caused by the incident on the business organization before it can be resolved. Urgency is how quickly incident resolution is required.

Incident Manager Recovery Run books/decision trees – A runbook or decision tree can be very valuable for a major incident management team that are more generalist. Runbook or decision trees can be built by a service SME and manager prior to an incident, which will provide the incident management team with valuable actions to take in the first 30 minutes while the experts are joining the bridge.

24/7 Persistent Chat Collaboration Room – When an incident occurs, it is critical to collaborate quickly with resources to determine how to diagnose and repair the system. With support resources spread out through a building, city, or even country, companies need a collaboration tool beyond just an email chain or audio bridge call. A 24/7 persistent chat collaboration room will allow resources from management, operations, development, storage, platform, network, and other areas to collaborate. This collaboration room will allow teams to hold real-time discussions. Resources joining the discussion in progress will be able to review the persistent chat history. Resources can visually share documents and files. A list of completed recovery steps and a visual timeline can be displayed. A list of the participants can be displayed, and the entire recovery event can be recorded for a post-incident review.

Major Incident Lifecycle – Recovery, Restoration, and Closure

Recovery is the segment to bring an IT service that has returned to a normal state. The overall business IT service made up of one or more configuration items may or may not be recovered at this point. Restoration is the point when the actual business service has been recovered, and the end-users are able to use the services successfully. Closure occurs after the service is available to the user and the recovery teams validate that the service is stable from immediate reoccurrence.

Major Incident Lifecycle – Recovery, Restoration, and Closure recommendations

Incident Resolution Category Scheme – Initial incident categories focus on what monitoring or the customer sees and experiences as an issue. Capturing incident resolution categories allows the incident owner to categorize the incident based on what the end resolution was based on all the information learned from recovering the system or how it was fixed. This is important for troubleshooting future incidents.

Root Cause Analysis – This is the process of determining what happened, why it happened, and what to do to reduce the likelihood that it will happen again. This process involves collecting the data, identifying all potential causes, determining the root cause, and implementing a fix, if possible, to eliminate the problem. A workaround may be necessary until the permanent fix has been implemented.

Post-Incident Review (PIR) – A PIR is an evaluation of the response and recovery actions during a major incident. The post-incident review identifies what went well and opportunities that exist to improve. It also finalizes the capture of the incident data for root cause analysis by problem management.

Post-Incident Review process

The Post Incident Review (PIR) process is an evaluation of the incident management response and recovery effort for the major, critical, and high priority incidents. The post-incident review meeting is initiated once the incident has been resolved. Therefore, information captured during the incident's lifecycle is saved for review. A post-incident review is a process to review the incident information from occurrence to closure. The output of the meeting is a report of potential findings detailing how the incident could have been handled better. For that reason, consistently performing post-incident reviews are a great way to improve the incident handling process continuously.

> **Post-Incident Review Goals**
>
> - Eliminate or reduce the risk of the incident to re-occur.
> - Improve the initial incident detection time.
> - Identify improvements needed to diagnose the incident including service impacted, priority level and the correct resolver teams to be engaged.
> - Review the repair steps and identify recommendations to reduce future incident repair duration.
> - Review the duration to initiate and complete activities with improvement recommendations as an output.
> - Ensure incident communication was proper or if any areas of improvement exist.

A post-incident review is like a football team reviewing game tapes to understand what went well and what can be improved for the next game. Ultimately, you do not want the incident ever to reoccur again. By identifying the precursors of the incident, processes and configurations can be changed to eliminate reoccurrence. If the incident does reoccur again, the post-incident review should have identified how to detect, diagnose, and repair the incident quicker and more efficiently.

Under the direction of the incident manager, all resources involved in the incident as needed will be part of the post-incident review. These resources are needed to create a timeline of actions during the incident. Each of the following resources can provide valuable information.

Post-Incident Review of Meeting Resources

For a post-incident review meeting to be successful, all the needed resources should be gathered. While not all resources may be available or are in the progress of being completed, the meeting should complete as much of the review as possible. Follow-up action items will also be assigned with the goal of completing a formal report.

> **Post-Incident Review meeting resources**
> - Incident Manager or delegate to run the post-incident review
> - Major incident manager or coordinator who ran the incident war room
> - Incident documentation including the ticket data, timelines and decisions made
> - Change ticket information, if applicable
> - All incident recovery resources involved
> - Event monitoring data
> - Application or system engineers
> - Problem management root cause analysis

Chapter 27

Service Requests

> **Chapter Objectives**
>
> - Define a service request and discuss how it is different than an incident.
> - Understand the service request fulfillment process.
> - Review how service level agreements work with service requests.
> - Discuss what a service catalog is and how it is used.
> - Provide the top service request best practices.

A Service Request is a process for your customers to request system access, information, or a standard low-risk change to be fulfilled. Let's break that down a little more. First, customers requesting access to an application, file system, or website is a service request. For example, if a customer needs access to a specific financial directory, they will contact the Help Desk to have this request fulfilled. Secondly, customers will call the Help Desk for basic or technical information. This information includes the "how do I" questions, technology-related tips, and general instructions. Finally, customers call the Help Desk for a standard change which is low risk and a common request for service. These standard changes include installing software, upgrading hardware, and ordering accessories.

What is the difference between Service Requests and Incidents?

A service request is different than an incident. As stated above, a service request is when a customer needs access, information, or a standard change. On the other hand, an incident can be described as something that is broken, and the customer needs it fixed. A technical definition for an incident is an event not part of the standard operation of the service, causing an interruption to the quality of the service.

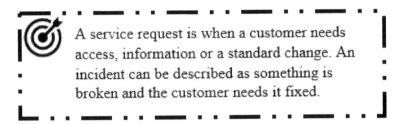

A service request is when a customer needs access, information or a standard change. An incident can be described as something is broken and the customer needs it fixed.

A ticket's average lifecycle duration is also different between a service request and an incident. For an incident ticket, when something is broken, a priority level is associated with driving resolution. The higher the priority, the quicker it must be resolved. A service request that is completed may be dependent on external variables such as parts in stock, equipment being ordered, and shipping durations, as examples. However, all the logistics to fulfill the request can be mapped out and given an expected time for the service to be delivered. For that reason, the service request fulfillment process is critical to understand.

Service Request Fulfillment

Service request fulfillment is the process of providing IT services and equipment to the customer. The IT service fulfillment process must be defined so repeatable steps are used by the Help Desk agents and other IT staff. A repeatable process will ensure customers receive the services requested in an expected timeframe. This will lead to high customer satisfaction. Ensure the fulfillment process is monitored until completion. Requests are tracked from beginning to end to ensure the services are provisioned in a timely manner. Provisioning timeframes are governed by Service Level Agreements (SLA). These SLAs are agreed to by IT and the customers, so both parties have the same expectations. SLAs are underpinned by Operational Level Agreements (OLA). OLAs are agreements IT has with vendors supplying parts and services used to fulfill the customer's service request.

Service Level Agreements

A service level agreement is a contract between the service provider and the customer. It defines the IT services to be provided by IT to their customers. It also states the time frame the IT service is to be provisioned. It identifies how to measure the effectiveness of the IT service fulfillment and how to report on it. If the service provider fails to meet the provisioning expectations, it details how it should be reported. Once reported, an SLA defines the response format and time frame the service provider is held to respond. It also defines the consequences the service provider could face in failure to deliver to expectations.

IT Service Catalog

Every Information Technology department will have some form of a list of services available to its customers. Mature departments will have an IT service catalog. In ITIL, an IT service catalog is a listing of IT services available for the customer to request. An IT service catalog presents IT services that are available for the customers in a centralized location. At many companies, you will find the service catalog as part of the corporate intranet website. A service catalog is a one-stop electronic shop for customers to find IT services. The service catalog will include information about the IT service. This information may include a description of the service, how to order the service, and the expected time the service will be delivered. Service catalogs have become very advanced. Many service catalogs will have backend workflow engines. A catalog workflow engine will handle the sequence of approval and provisioning steps through which a service request passes from initiation to completion.

Your Help Desk ticketing application may have a module to start your catalog. In addition, there are many IT service catalog software vendors with extensive options and features. The IT service catalog contains two views based on your role. For the customer, there is a customer view. For the IT or Help Desk staff, there is a technical view. Both views have specific purposes, and they work together to fulfill IT service requests.

IT Service Catalog Customer View - The customer view of your IT service catalog is the public-facing view. This is where your customers can browse and initiate a request for a new IT service. Remember, the customer view is geared toward the customer and the business services they want. The IT service catalog customer view will include information about IT services. Each IT service will include a description, cost, ordering information, and expected service delivery times.

IT Service Catalog Technical View - The technical view of your IT service catalog is the internal IT facing view. This is where the internal IT staff can list and maintain a new IT service.

Service Request Best Practices

IT services requested by your customers are common and frequent. The work of provisioning those IT services is highly repeatable. Due to this fact, systematically removing motion waste and fulfillment inefficiencies can improve the quality and speed of delivery of the IT service requested. To set up an effective and customer-focused service request fulfillment process, you must focus on some key issues. These key issues or best practices will ensure your fulfillment process meets customer expectations.

Focus on the most frequently requested services - You should start building your request fulfillment processes by focusing on the services most frequently requested. Start by looking at your Help Desk ticketing system. The benefit of starting with the requests with the most volume is you have a lot of history delivering these services. Furthermore, you will receive the biggest benefit in improving the efficiency of high-volume requests. Every request for service needs to have a corresponding ticket created and correctly categorized. Running reports on ticket categories and volumes can provide great data on which services to start on.

Focus on being customer-centric - Your list of IT services available must be understood by the customer. In your list, use terms to describe the service which the customers can understand. When building your service catalog, the IT service descriptions should not be written for IT staff but for a general user. Remove excessive technical jargon and make sure the IT services listed are reviewed by customer focus groups.

Make it self-service - Third, ensure FAQs are available for your customers to find answers to their questions. One of the major benefits of having an IT service catalog is your customers become more self-sufficient. If customers can navigate a service catalog and request services on their own, it will free up IT resources for other activities. The request fulfillment process should also be as automated as possible. Consider building a service catalog with a backend workflow system.

Centralize requests – The best practice for service requests is to ensure to centralize your service requests. Your Help Desk should be the single point of contact for all requested services. This may also include administrative, facility, and other types of requests. By having a single point of contact for your customers, there will not be any confusion on where to go to initiate and check the status of requests.

Chapter 28

Event Management

> **Chapter Objectives**
> - Learn the types of events.
> - Understand what event management is.
> - Review the objectives of event management.
> - Learn when event management is used and how it works.
> - Understand the benefits of event management.

What is an event?

An event is defined as a change of state of an IT system that is detected, recorded, and is a significant occurrence for the IT infrastructure.

Types of events

There are three types of events. The three types of events are informational, warning, and exception.

Informational event - The first type of event we will discuss is an informational event. As the name suggests, these events are status informing only, and they do not require immediate action or response. Informational events are used to confirm that an activity or process occurred, finished, or was successfully run. One example of this is if a backup of an IT system is completed. It's important to know that that backup is completed, but no further action is needed.

Warning event - The next type of event is a warning. A warning is a notification that something is about to occur, and action should be taken by a team supporting it. Usually, a warning is generated because a threshold or a condition is about to be reached.

Exception event - The third type of event is an exception. An exception means that something being monitored has breached a threshold. Whereas a warning event is notifying that a threshold breach could occur, an exception event is a significant occurrence because a breach did occur. One example of an exception is the backup of a server that did not run. It also could be that the backup failed.

What is event management?

Event management is the process of monitoring IT services to ensure they are performing well. IT services are made up of hardware, software, and applications. IT services will break down or have problems. With so many IT systems in a data center, it would be hard to track all events manually. That's where event management steps in. Event management will monitor the processes running on all those IT systems and alert you if there is a problem. These alerts coming in will normally go to your help desk ticketing application. In that application, they will create a helpdesk ticket. They helped us will review the ticket in the sign of priority into the group to look into it.

Objectives of the event management process

The objectives of the event management process are all related to notifying IT staff of the health and performance status of IT services being monitored. If the health or performance of an IT service deviates from expectations, then an event is generated. Below are the specific objectives of an event management program.

1 – IT services and configurations will be monitored and will have a normal operating baseline measurement established. Event trigger thresholds will be set. If the IT service or configuration items experience a significant operational change, and it is detected, then an event is logged.

2 – Operational information is captured with an event, response actions are recorded, and support teams receive all related data of the event.

3 – Able to compare current performance to the desired performance

4 – Acts as an input for other processes such as incident management.

5 – Used for continuous improvement, reporting, and operational processes.

Where is event management used?

IT services - Event management can be used to monitor the health and performance of IT services.

Security - Event management can be used to monitor systems for intrusions or security-related actions. This could be several failed login attempts. This could also be unwarranted access to certain systems.

Data Center Environment - Event management is used to monitor the environment of the data center and the main systems that control the environment. The environment must stay cool so that temperatures will be monitored. This includes monitoring for high or low humidity. Event management can work with the fire protection system to monitor for fire or smoke.

So how does event management work?

Event management works by having probes deployed to the systems being monitored. These probes will work with system logging and resource measuring processes to monitor activity such as CPU utilization, storage size, and many other things. In the event management application, you will configure thresholds for each of those systems. While monitoring, if a process goes above a threshold, an action can be taken. These actions can include creating an alert and initiating a response or some other type of action. If your threshold is set too low, you will generate many alerts, which will mask the real problem alerts. If the thresholds are set too high, you'll never see the problem. Event management requires a lot of tuning of the system to be effective.

Benefits of event management

Decreased incident response time - Event management can help you respond to incidents faster. Instead of an end-user experiencing an issue and then reporting it, event monitoring can instantly generate an incident ticket. This is important since a major incident can take down your business and cause financial, brand, or security concerns. The quicker you respond to an incident, the faster you can recover it. As a result, the downtime of an IT system will be reduced, making the IT system more available.

Automation of incident recovery - Event management can help you automate areas of your IT services. Event management is based on a system of workflows. If X occurs, then do Y. This action and response are what make event management so powerful. If a storage system is reaching a capacity threshold, more storage can be added automatically. If a server is running out of CPU processing percentage, more CPU processing can automatically be added. Meanwhile, everything is logged, and appropriate personnel can be notified.

Event management challenges

Alert overload - Even small and medium-sized companies may have hundreds of servers in their data center. These servers could have hundreds of applications running on them. Each server also has an operating system. Most servers are attached to storage and the network. As you can imagine, if event management is not set up properly, you could have thousands of alerts generated each day. It's important to filter and suppress non-relevant alerts. Then relevant alerts can be acted on with the non-relevant alerts filtered and suppressed.

Correlation of alerts - With thousands of alerts, how do you know what the alerts mean? It's important that you can correlate an alert to an issue. You must understand what that issue is before you can start to fix it. The event management application will have many configurations you can set up to understand and program what are alert means when it happens. You also must have trained staff able to set that up and understand the system.

Chapter 29

Problem Management

> **Chapter Objectives**
>
> - Learn what is a problem.
> - Understand what problem management is.
> - Review reactive and proactive problem management.
> - Learn what a work around and a known error is.
> - Understand the KPIs of problem management.

One of the more overlooked ITIL processes is problem management. Many companies implementing ITIL will focus on incident and change management first. What companies realize after implementing incident and change management is that they need a problem management program to improve the overall availability of IT services. A mature program managing problems will lead to preventing reoccurring incidents or at least reducing the impact. Focusing on problems in your environment will increase the uptime of your IT services. Therefore, problem management is a critical component of your overall IT Service Management program. For these reasons, the Help Desk must be an active player to be successful.

The Help Desk plays a major role in managing incidents and problems. Accurate and thorough incident ticket documentation by the Help

Desk will significantly help the root cause analysis of incident generating problems. Assigning correct ticket categories to incident tickets by the Help Desk will improve problem identification. Correct ticket category assignment will significantly improve incident matching, ticket type trending, and identifying problem candidates. For these reasons, you need to understand what a problem is.

What is a Problem?

A problem is the main source of a fault in the IT infrastructure. A problem can cause one or more incidents that impact IT services. Incidents are a result of the problem, and the end-users experience unstable, degraded, or unavailable IT services. You will hear the term root cause to describe the underlying cause of an incident. A problem's root cause will have to be identified before it can be fixed. A problem ticket is raised based on the incident or incidents which caused the fault and possibly operational outage. When a problem has been defined, it can be called a known error. A known error is a problem where the root cause has been identified and a workaround is in place. Once a solution is found to fix the problem permanently, a change request is created and implemented to resolve the problem,

What is Problem Management?

Problem management is the life cycle process of identifying, investigating, documenting, and permanently eliminating related incidents from the production environment. Incident management is focused on restoring an IT service quickly through any means. Problem management is focused on identifying the incident's root cause and preventing the recurrence of additional service-impacting incidents. Problems are resolved by defining and implementing a solution to the problem. The solution to the problem is implemented by a change request. In a ticketing application, a problem management investigation ticket is created from an incident ticket or operational outage. This process creates an association between the incident and problem tickets. In most instances, there is more than one incident related to a problem. In those cases, all the incidents should be linked to the problem ticket.

Problem Management: Reactive and Proactive.

Problem management focuses on problems that cause incidents or may cause incidents in the future. Therefore, a problem investigation can be initiated both reactively and proactively. Reactive problem management is initiated after one or more incidents occur. The reactive problem investigation will focus on finding the incident's root cause, defining a workaround, and ultimately implementing a solution through the change management process. Proactive problem management focuses on preventing future incidents before they occur. This is accomplished by initiating preventative problem investigations. These problem investigations will focus on analyzing operational data, configurations, and system performance data, looking for potential problems. For example, if an application running on a server has above average CPU utilization for an extended period of time, there may be a potential problem. Investigating the reason why the CPU utilization is high before a customer-impacting incident occurs is being proactive.

Problem Management Work Around

A workaround may be developed when a problem has been investigated and the root cause found but not fixed. A workaround is when a full resolution is not yet available for an incident or problem, but something can be done to allow the user to complete their task. At times a solution cannot be defined for permanently resolving incident-causing problems. In those cases, problem management will attempt to minimize the impact of the problem with a workaround. In this situation, the problem is identified as a known error. These known errors are published by problem management in a known error database until a time when a permanent solution becomes available.

Known Error Database

Companies implementing problem management may realize a significant reduction in call handle time and first contact resolution. This is achieved by implementing a known error database, which is a key component of problem management. A known error database is an invaluable tool for the Help Desk to help end-users remain productive using IT services. When the Help Desk receives a contact about something broken, one place they check is if the issue is identified in the known error database. If the reported issue has been identified as a known error, the Help Desk agent can implement the published workaround. Implementing a workaround will allow users to continue to work at some level while a permanent solution to the problem is being developed.

Help Desk and problem management

There are many benefits to the Help Desk and customers from implementing an effective problem management program. Not only will there be an improved quality of IT Services but also repeat incident occurrences should be eliminated. The Help Desk staff plays a significant role in problem management activities. Day in and day out, the Help Desk deals with hundreds or thousands of incident tickets. Usually, Incident Management will be engaged for more significantly impacting incidents and a large spike of similar issues. In those cases, the incident manager will create a problem ticket once the incident is resolved. If the incident results in a workaround, the known error database will be updated with details of the workaround. The Help Desk staff become in tune with trends of customer break-fix issues. A Help Desk agent may be able to identify when customers are reporting similar issues which could be related to an underlying problem that needs to be addressed. When the Help Desk sees similar reported incidents over a longer period, they may create a proactive problem ticket for review. Finally, your organization will become proactive in identifying and eliminating infrastructure problems.

What are the KPIs of Problem Management?

Being able to report on key performance indicators for problem management is important. There are a lot of metrics that can be used. The most important thing to remember is that your problem management program should use a robust ticketing application to manage problems. The problem template should have many fields to capture data. By capturing a lot of information about each problem as they move through the problem lifecycle, current and future reporting will be robust. Since there are so many ways to pull data and report on problems, we have grouped some of the most common below.

The number of problems reported – These types of reports focus on the number of problems managed by the problem management program. These reports are based on different quantity totals of problems. The benefit of these types of reports will give you in site into the trend of problem occurrence. Knowing the number of problems at various stages of the problem lifecycle will allow management to manage the backlog of problems, become more efficient, and ultimately reduce the overall occurrence. Each of the below reports can be further filtered by date, severity, and other attributes.

Total number of problems
Total number of active problems
Total number of resolved problems
Total number of closed problems

Duration of problems reporting - These types of reports focus on the duration of problems managed by the problem management program. These duration-type reports do not just focus on the time from open to close but categorize problems by lifecycle segments. The benefit of these types of reports will give you insight into the effectiveness of the problem management team processing the problems to closure. Below are the most common problem time segments in order of typical occurrence.

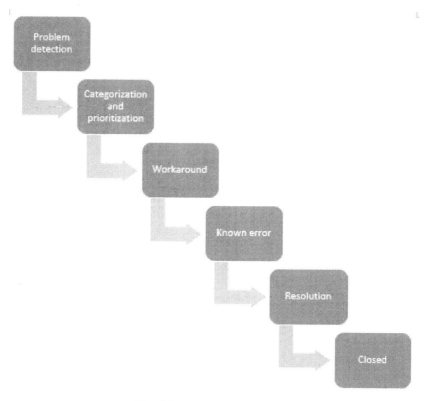

Problem management steps

Attributes of problems - These types of reports focus on specific attributes of problems managed by the problem management program. These types of reports look at specific attributes or characteristics of problems. The benefit of these types of reports will give insight into specific and related areas of your problem management program. Below are the most common problem attributes tracked and reported.
- A report on the percentage of problems where a root cause has been completed can be useful.
- Problems that reoccurred and SLA compliance are common areas tracked and reported.

Problem Management Worksheet

Step 1 – Prioritizing problem management investigation candidates:

A problem investigation is initiated by identifying IT service issue candidates. Problem management candidates can be identified by any or all the following methods.

- Mandatory for Priority 1 incidents and highly recommended for Priority 2 incidents that caused a recent service degradation or outage.
- Technical staff, including Help Desk Agents, level 2, level 3 resolver teams, developers, application owners, and management, nominating problem candidates.
- Customer and business partners reporting critical service-impacting issues.
- A proactive Incident trend analysis.

Step 2 – Gather the data:

Once the problem management investigation candidate has been identified, it is important to gather the foundational data about the problem.

If a service outage occurs, develop a timeline of events for prior, during, and after the outage. The Help Desk can assist with a large amount of this data.

- Gather and assess error, diagnostic, and monitoring information.
- Gather the number of Incidents related to the Problem
- Review the frequency of this problem by searching the Help Desk ticket data.
- Was a change recently implemented that could have caused this problem?

Step 3 – Form a problem review team

Identify the needed technical staff, Help Desk Agents, and customer representatives need to meet and review the following quickly:

- Review all available foundational problem data.
- Identify likely causes.
- Discuss any contributing factors.
- Eliminate likely causes until you have the most probable cause remaining.
- Identify the root cause.

Step 4 – Propose and implement a solution

- Document a Request for Change for any action you intend on taking to resolve the issue.
- Submit a Request for Change or implement solutions that do not require Change management.

Step 5 – Validate the fix

- Confirm success/failure of Approved Change.
- Have the customer validate the problem does not occur anymore. Monitor Help Desk tickets for future re-occurrences.

Chapter 30

Change Management

Chapter Objectives

Change Management

- Define what a request for change is.
- Identify the types of changes.
- Understand how to manage change risk.
- Learn the roles of change management.
- Define and measure success.
- Review key performance indicators for change management.

In IT Service Management there is a process called change management. Change management is based on the ITIL framework. The change management process standardizes changes to the IT infrastructure by managing the change lifecycle. Standardizing the change management process is important to be efficient and accurate. Standardizing the change management will also minimize the negative impact on customers, IT services, and operations. Having a rigorous change control process is an important factor to be considered in having a mature IT operation. Following a structured change process also allows the changes to be scheduled to avoid multiple change implementations being in conflict. Prioritizing changes will make sure that changes with the highest priority will be implemented first.

Request for Change (RFC)

Changes to IT infrastructure are initiated through the Request for Change (RFC) process. The request for change form is a formal request for the implementation of a change. The request for change form provides all the information required to review and approve changes. Requests for change can be initiated for several different reasons.

Reactive to incidents - Changes can be initiated to eliminate problems in the IT environment which has failed and caused incidents.

Proactively prevent incidents – A change can be implemented to eliminate potential problems in the IT environment before it fails and cause incidents.

Compatibility changes – A change is initiated because an associated service has or will change. The change focuses on keeping a system compatible with the associated system.

Capability enhancement - Changes can be initiated by the business as part of deploying, upgrading, removing, or configuring IT services and applications.

Operational changes – Low-risk routine changes are initiated during normal operational activities.

Type of Changes

Standard Change – A standard change is a low-risk change that occurs frequently and has a low probability of failing. A standard change is a pre-approved change that follows a standardized implementation process. Since they are pre-approved, they do not need additional change management approval. However, if a standard type change starts causing incident trends, they will be reviewed to modify or revoke the standard classification.

Normal Change – A normal change is a change that follows a normal process flow. The change request requires approval from approvers associated with the impacted system, the change management team, and the Change Advisory Board (CAB).

Emergency Change - A change needs to resolve an outage or a pending outage associated with an incident. The incidents that drive emergency changes are the most likely critical or high priority under the incident management direction. Approval of the emergency change requires approval by on-call senior leadership and the change manager or designate.

Managing to change risk

The customer expects their IT services to be stable and be available to perform their function without unexpected results. Customers also want their IT services to evolve with their changing business requirements. When we say evolve, it means the IT services may require one or more changes to upgrade functionality, enhance service, and improve stability. Changing IT services introduces risk. A failed, partially successful, or poorly designed change may impact stability. As an IT professional, minimizing risk when introducing a change is critical.

When a change request is created, risk must be assessed. Initially, the risk is assessed by incorporating a risk calculator. A risk calculator is part of the change request form. It asks a series of questions to help the change requestor assign a risk level to the change. Through the series of questions, the changing risk can be quantified by the impact it will have on the services and the probability of the change failing. The following are examples of questions to assess the risk level.

Does the change impact more than X amount of people?

Does the change affect more than one location or site?
Does this change need to be done during business hours?
Will this change be performed outside of the established maintenance windows?
Do you have a backout plan for this change?

Change management roles

As with all ITIL processes, there are defined roles and responsibilities in change management.

Change Manager - This is the process owner for change management. As a process owner, the change manager has the responsibility to ensure the change process is following the approved change management process. The primary responsibilities are defined as;

Ensure the officially approved change management procedures are current and available to everyone involved in the change management process. Ensure everyone involved in the change process has been trained.

Ensures that all change-related activities are being performed as per the established change procedure.

It is the principle that facilitates the change advisory board and their meetings to review higher impact changes.

Change Coordinator – A change coordinator is part of the change management team and has delegated authority from the change manager to review and process change requests and other associated activities.

Change Advisory Board (CAB) – Technical experts, leaders, and decision-makers can comprise the makeup of a change advisory board. This is a group of people with the responsibility to review changes to the IT environment. They have the authority to approve, reject, or request additional information on proposed change requests. The CAB is led by the change manager, who ensures the appropriate staff members are involved, and processes are followed.

Change Requestor – The change requestor completes the initial change request and provides all the documentation needed to review and process it. Typically, the requestor of a proposed change request will represent it at the CAB meeting and answer questions related to the change.

Change Approvers – When a change is proposed to an IT system, approval is needed from specific stakeholders of the impacted system. The specific change approvers are based on the specific system. Examples of change approvers can be application owners, business leaders, and IT groups such as databases, networks, or other areas depending on the system being changed.

IT Change management: Measuring Success

Change management activity on IT services can cause instability, service outages, and faults that generate incidents. All this change activity and resulting data can feed into Key Performance Indicator (KPI) reporting tools. KPI reports are the raw data for a specific measurement. There are so many available change management KPI metrics to measure change management processes that you may become overwhelmed. Many companies will publish daily, weekly, monthly, and annual KPI reports. These raw KPI reports may be useful to IT management in monitoring how the IT change management process is performing. The business and customers typically want to receive reports at a higher summary level. Individual KPI reports tend to be over-detailed and very specific to the point where management and the business may not find them useful. Customers value reports that summarize the status of IT services to validate if they are stable, highly available, and error-free after upgrades and customizations are applied. With so many KPIs available to us, how do we produce reports to let us know if our IT change management process is successful? Is the IT change management process achieving the outcome we are striving to achieve?

IT Change management Critical Success Factors (CSF)

By combining specific KPI reports and summarizing them as groups, we can determine if we are meeting the IT change management outcomes we desire. We can determine our outcomes by building Critical Success Factors (CSF). Every company and department has different values of what outcomes of IT change management are most important. To start building CSFs, you need to meet with stakeholders such as IT engineers, business partners, IT management, and possibly customers. Listen to their feedback and understand what is working and what may need improvement. Examples of improvement areas that may need a CSF are;

Change quality – A CSF for change quality is focused on the effectiveness and efficiency of each phase of a change request lifecycle. A company could have an overall change quality CSF for the entire change life-cycle process. However, the most effective change quality CSF would allow the ability to drill into each phase. One or more CSFs could be created for the following change request life-cycle phases.

> **Change request life-cycle phases**
>
> - Change request forms – Measurements can focus the number of change request reworks and reason codes for rework.
> - Successful implementation plans
> - Change communications
> - Change validation testing
> - Change back out plans
> - Changes that cause incident and outages.

Specific KPI reports used to build a CSF for change quality could include feedback surveys, outage reports, change needing backup restores, unsuccessful change data, number of incidents, and such.

Change duration – A CSF group for change duration is focused on the time and energy into creating, processing, approving, and scheduling request for changes. The overall change duration measurement includes the total time from opening the change request to closing the change after implementation. An effective change quality CSF should also allow the drilling into the durations between each phase of the change request lifecycle. Being able to drill into the duration of each phase can uncover where the process is constrained.

IT Change management Key Performance Indicators (KPIs)

Feedback surveys
Post-change and related incident feedback surveys can point to issues with the change management process. Obtaining both a rating score and comments will provide very useful data for making improvements.

Change request backlog
Change request status is currently in the initial request to implementation stages. Reporting on the number, percentage, and current stage of backlogged change requests is very useful. Backlogged change requests can identify resource constraints and process bottlenecks that need to be reviewed.

Average change completion duration
This is a measurement of the average change completion duration measured between the initial change request and change closure. Useful variations include duration between stages such as initial request, approved, scheduled, implemented, and closed. Also, measuring the change completion duration by the change type, risk level, and IT system category can be useful.

IT service outages caused by a change
The outages caused by a change metric are the percentage of changes causing IT service outages due to the implementation of planned changes. IT service outages should include unplanned outages. Variations of outage data could include number, percentage, and duration.

Urgent change data
Ideally, you want all changes to follow the standard change process. Expediting a change request as an urgent change increases the potential risk of the change failing or creating quality and performance issues.

Unplanned outage due to changes
Changes to IT services routinely include planned outages to IT services during the change window. Unplanned outages mean that the IT service becomes unavailable or degraded due to the change and was not expected. Unplanned outages due to changes generate incidents and can be measured.

Unauthorized change activity

Unauthorized change activity is a significant risk factor. All infrastructure and IT service changes must be managed through the change management process. An unauthorized change can be detected through the consolidation of the Configuration Management Database (CMDB). A change in infrastructure for which there is not a change registered is considered unauthorized.

Changes scheduled outside the maintenance window
Implementing changes during a maintenance window for an IT service introduces less risk. A maintenance window is an agreed reoccurring period of time where IT and the business plan for IT service downtime.

Backed-out changes
If a change has issues being implemented completely or fails the validation testing, the change may need to be backed out. Measuring the number of changes that were rolled back relative versus successful changes is a good measurement of the change process. A good practice is to understand what percent of change requests need to be backed out and why. This can lead to many change improvement projects and a mature process.

Incidents caused by changes
If a change causes one or more incidents, it is important to associate incident tickets with the change record. Understanding what changes caused incidents will make it possible to identify specific change issues needing to be addressed. Through continuous improvement initiatives, these issues can be corrected. This will lead to a reduction of unplanned interruptions or degradation of IT services.

Rate of change activity
Is the volume of change requests growing? What periods of time is the busiest? Measure the number of changes opened and closed in a given time period.

Chapter 31

Knowledge Management

> **Chapter Objectives**
>
> - Understand what needs to be completed to improve knowledge management.
> - Learn the step by step knowledge improvement process.
>   - Step 1 Identify
>   - Step 2 Collect
>   - Step 3 Create
>   - Step 4 Define roles and responsibilities
>   - Step 5 Format
>   - Step 6 Training
>   - Step 7 Use
>   - Step 8 Improve

When a customer contacts your Help Desk with a service question or issue, you expect your Help Desk Agents to provide consistent, repeatable, and accurate solutions. If the needed service support information is scattered throughout your company, how can you expect your Help Desk Agents to provide timely support? Knowledge management is the process of using service support knowledge to resolve a customer's service question or issue. Knowledge management systems make service support information immediately available to your agents to answer the customer's questions or resolve their service issues on the first contact. A robust and mature knowledge management system enables the Help Desk to deliver greater business value with more efficiency. We have outlined a process of starting or maturing a knowledge management system.

The knowledge management improvement process overview

Step 1 Identify – Select your initial list of IT services needing knowledge management solution updates based on priority and frequency.

Step 2 Collect – Gather knowledge management documentation for the identified services.

Step 3 Create – Establish and define your knowledge management solution repository.

Step 4 Define roles and responsibilities – Define knowledge management roles and responsibilities.

Step 5 Format – Define a consistent template format for your knowledge management solutions.

Step 6 Training - Help Desk Agent training and coaching.

Step 7 Use – Place your knowledge management system into production.

Step 8 Improve – Continuous improvement efforts for your knowledge management system.

The knowledge management improvement process detailed steps

Step 1 - Identify knowledge management services

It can be overwhelming starting or maturing a knowledge management system with a substantial number of IT services your department supports. It is important to target your knowledge management improvement efforts to your highest priority IT services first. Create a list of all the services you provide support for by talking to your staff, customers, management, and other key groups. You can also query your ticketing application for the listing of support types offered. Once you have a list of all your services, create a column called "priority" and assign a priority rating of high, medium, and low based on how critical the service is to your company's business. Next, create another column called "frequency" and assign a rating of high, medium, and low based on the monthly customer contacts for questions or issues related to each service.

> **Action Steps**
>
> **Target knowledge management service candidates**
>
> 1. Create a list of all the services the Help Desk provides support for.
> 2. Create a column called "priority" and assign a priority rating of high, medium, and low based on how critical the service is to your company's business.
> 3. Create a column called "frequency" and assign a priority rating of high, medium, and low based on the monthly customer contacts for questions or issues related to each service.
>
> | Service | Priority | Frequency |
> |---------|----------|-----------|
> | | | |
> | | | |
> | | | |

Step 2 - Collect knowledge management solutions

Start with the top 10 services on your list that have a high priority to resolve and have a high frequency of contact volume. Focusing on the top 10 services will keep your team focused and help you refine the process. Collect all the support information you can find related to these top 10 services. You can find support information with your staff, the application development teams, customers, and the Internet, just to name a few. Save each solution to a document. These solutions may be raw data, partial solutions, and information that will need to be refined in future steps. Store these solution documents into a specific folder for the service. The file storage system will not need to be fancy since this is just temporary storage until a knowledge repository is created.

Step 3 - Create your knowledge management repository

There are many options for what repository to use for your knowledge management system solutions. The first option is to investigate if your Help Desk ticketing system has a module for knowledge management. Using the knowledge module in your Help Desk ticketing system is typically your best option. However, if your system does not have a knowledge management module or the module will not work well for you, I suggest setting up a Wiki. A wiki is a web-based service, which solutions can upload, edit, and remove. In a wiki, you can create hyperlinks that will allow your Help Desk agents to click between the support solution pages. You can host a wiki internally or find a vendor to host it externally. The most important attributes of the knowledge management repository you select are that the system presents solutions quickly to reduce customer delays and all of the content is full text indexed to allow Help Desk Agents to search by keywords as needed.

Step 4 - Define Knowledge management roles

A knowledge management system can quickly become bloated with excessive solutions. These solutions can be on pages not following your standards. A knowledge management system can also have outdated and incorrect solutions if a role and responsibility structure is not defined. Also, it is very important to open a solution review process to developers, business analysts, and escalation teams for expert review. We recommend the following knowledge management roles be defined.

Knowledge Management process owner – This role is responsible for the knowledge management process. This includes knowledge management procedures, documentation, and rules. This person initiates or accepts process change requests, organizes group reviews of process change requests, implements process changes, and ensures communication occurs on process changes.

Knowledge Management Administrator – This role is responsible for access control and the proper function of the knowledge management repository server and database.

Knowledge Editor – This role is responsible for the final review, approval, and publishing of new or updated knowledge management solutions. The knowledge editor coordinates logical structure changes to the known solution structure.

Knowledge Submitter – Gathers knowledge information and proposes new or updated knowledge solutions.

Knowledge User – Uses knowledge solutions to provide support to the customer.

Step 5 - Format your knowledge management solutions

Once you have identified a knowledge management repository, collected knowledge management solutions, and defined roles, it is time to format your knowledge management structure.

Basic knowledge base structure - The basic knowledge base structure I recommend is as follows. At the main level of your knowledge base structure, you have the knowledge base home page. The knowledge base home page is your main starting point when searching for knowledge. The knowledge base home page will display the name of each of your IT services and will have a link to the service home page. A service home page is the main page for that service. It describes what the service is and how it is used. It will display many attributes about the service, such as URL, current version, and known issues. The service home page will have links to all the related knowledge solutions. The service solutions are all organized under the service home page. Looking at the graphic for the basic knowledge base structure, you can see how the associations between the pages are arranged.

Basic Knowledge Base Structure

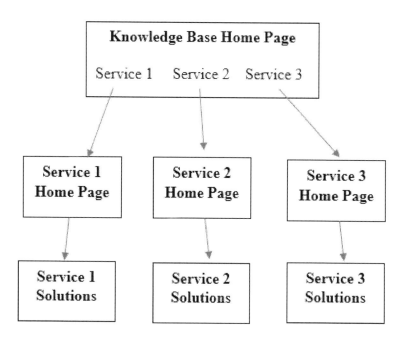

Service home page – The service home page will display all the attributes of the service. This service home page is to give the knowledgeable user an overview of all the key information about the service.

```
┌─────────────────────────────────────────┐
│           Service Home Page             │
│                                         │
│    Service name:                        │
│    Service description:                 │
│    Service level and priority:          │
│    Service URL:                         │
│    Current version:                     │
│    Service owner:                       │
│    Company/department:                  │
│    Service tier 1, 2, and 3 support teams: │
│    Service ticket classification:       │
│    Service maintenance window:          │
│    Known issues:                        │
│    Links to support solution pages:     │
│                                         │
└─────────────────────────────────────────┘
```

Service solution page – A service solution page is an article used to describe the solution for an issue. A service solution page is also used for specific support activities, such as how to install the application and support the service. There could be many individual service solution pages underneath the service solution homepage. I suggest that you create a template for the service solution pages. Having a template will keep the look and feel of the service solution pages consistent between all your solutions. This will make it easier for the user of the knowledge base to read and find the information quickly. All service solution pages should have knowledge base feedback tools from the user. Examples of these tools are the following.

Was this helpful rating – Allow the knowledge user the ability to acknowledge if the solution was helpful by offering a prompt on each solution.

Favorite bookmark – Sometimes, the knowledge user will want to bookmark the solution as a favorite. This is a common action when the solution is helpful and includes complex, detailed solution steps that may be difficult to remember.

Feedback memo – This allows the knowledge users the option to write a feedback memo to the knowledge team. Feedback can include tips or ideas on how to improve the solution.

Step 6 - Provide knowledge management training

It is important that each member of the knowledge management team, including the knowledge base user, receives training on the knowledge base system. Training will improve the adoption of the knowledge management system and ultimately improve the support the Help Desk offers. Common training topics include the following.

- Why use the knowledge management system.
- Users will need training on how to access the knowledge management system.
- How to search, use, and provide feedback on knowledge solutions.
- Users will need training on how to submit a new or updated solution for review.

In addition to training, the knowledge management system should have a way for knowledge users to view FAQs and step-by-step guides on using the system.

Step 7 - Use your knowledge management system

At this point, it is time to use your knowledge management system. You might not have knowledge management solutions entered for all services yet. However, by starting with mission-critical and high contact volume services, you will have the main services completed.

Only by using the knowledge management system will you be able to identify issues.

Step 8 - Improve your knowledge management system

As you use the knowledge management system, you will identify structure or solution updates that will be needed. If the Help Desk agent is unable to answer a question or solve an issue, they will escalate it to the next level of support. A good way to identify when solutions need to be updated is to monitor ticket escalations. Making sure the escalation groups provide good ticket notes or direct feedback on what they did to solve the issue is very important. They review the ticket detail and the notes from the escalation group. Based on that information, they then update the solution as needed.

Help Desk Resources and Important Links

Important Link: Help Desk Management Companion Resource Website. https://buildahelpdesk.com/help-desk-management-book/

Important Link: IT Help Desk Maturity Assessment Guide
https://buildahelpdesk.com/help-desk-maturity-assessment-guide/

Printed in Poland
by Amazon Fulfillment
Poland Sp. z o.o., Wrocław